WALKS AND TREKS
IN THE MARITIME ALPS

About the Author

Gillian Price was born in England but moved to Australia when young. After taking a degree in anthropology and working in adult education, she set off to travel through Asia and trek the Himalayas. The culmination of her journey was Venice where, her enthusiasm fired for mountains, the next logical step was towards the Dolomites, only hours away. Starting there, Gillian is steadily exploring the mountain ranges of Italy and bringing them to life for visitors in a series of outstanding guides for Cicerone.

When not out walking and photographing with Nicola, her Venetian cartographer husband, Gillian works as a freelance journalist and translator (www.gillianprice.eu). An adamant promoter of the use of public transport to minimise impact in Alpine areas, Gillian is an active member of the Italian Alpine Club and the Outdoor Writers and Photographers Guild.

Other Cicerone guides by the author
Walking in the Dolomites
Walking in the Central Italian Alps
Walking in Tuscany
Walking in Sicily
Shorter Walks in the Dolomites
Treks in the Dolomites: Alta Via 1 & 2 (co-author)
Walking on Corsica
Trekking in the Apennines – the Grande Escursione Appenninica (GEA)
Through the Italian Alps – the Grande Traversata delle Alpi (GTA)
Across the Eastern Alps: E5
Gran Paradiso: Alta Via 2 Trek and Day Walks
Italy's Sibillini National Park

WALKS AND TREKS
IN THE MARITIME ALPS

by
Gillian Price

2 POLICE SQUARE, MILNTHORPE, CUMBRIA LA7 7PY
www.cicerone.co.uk

Printed by MCC Graphics, Spain
A catalogue record for this book is available from the British Library.
Photographs by Gillian Price

Dedication

To little Bet and Dave, always a great inspiration!

Acknowledgements

My appetite for the divine Maritimes had been whetted on the GTA trek, so I didn't need much persuading when Nanni Villani of the Parco Naturale delle Alpi Marittime suggested I introduce the *anglosassoni* to the delights of these Mediterranean-scented mountains. Luckily Jonathan agreed to publish!

It goes without saying – but still warrants writing – that I truly appreciate the companionship and support of my beloved Nick on this, 'another', guidebook.

The company of the Story family was also enjoyed on some of these marvellous pathways.

Front cover: Lake in Valrossa (Walk 12, Stage 2)

CONTENTS

INTRODUCTION
The Maritime Alps 11
Walking 12
Rock Engravings 14
Wildflowers 16
Wildlife 18
Exploring the Maritime Alps 23
Information. 32
Access 34
When to Go 34
Accommodation. 36
Dos and Don'ts 39
What to Take 42
Maps 43
Emergencies 44
Using this Guide. 45

WALKS
1   Fontanalba Rock Engravings Circuit 47
2   Mont Bégo Loop 51
3   Vallée de la Roya to Vallée de Vésubie. 60
4   Upper Vallée de la Gordolasque 83
5   Lacs de Prals Circuit. 88
6   Ancient Passes above Madone de Fenestre 92
7   Vallon du Haut Boréon Circuit. 98
8   Lacs Bessons 99
9   Around the Argentera. 105
10 Lac des Adus Loop. 121
11 The Great Lakes Tour 125
12 The Alpi Marittime Trek 135
13 The Valasco Tour 160
14 The Fremamorta Loop 165
15 Rifugio Bozano 169
16 Rifugio Remondino and Lago di Nasta 173
17 Vallone di Lourousa 176

18 Traversing Colle di Fenestrelle 180
19 Rifugio Pagari Loop 185
20 Vallon del Vei del Bouc 193
21 Gorge della Reina 198
22 Vallone degli Alberghi 202
23 Costa di Planard 207
24 The Border Forts. 210

Appendix 1: French–English and Italian–English Glossaries 215
Appendix 2: Walk Summary Table 219

Map Key

═══════════	road
━━━━━━━━━━	walk route
- - - - - - - - - -	variant route
▬ ▪ ▬ ▪ ▬ ▪ ▬	park boundary
▮ ▯ ▮ ▯ ▮ ▯ ▮	international boundary
～～◯～～	river/lake
--------------------	tunnel
++++++++++++++++	railway

⬭	glacier	▲	peak
Ⓢ	start point	⚲	chapel/church
Ⓕ	finish point	≍	pass
⒮⒡	start/finish point	⌓	bivouac hut
❶	walk number	→	route direction arrow
○	town/village	→	direction arrow
▣	parking	ᛟ	old fort
⬆	refuge or hotel	✳	viewpoint

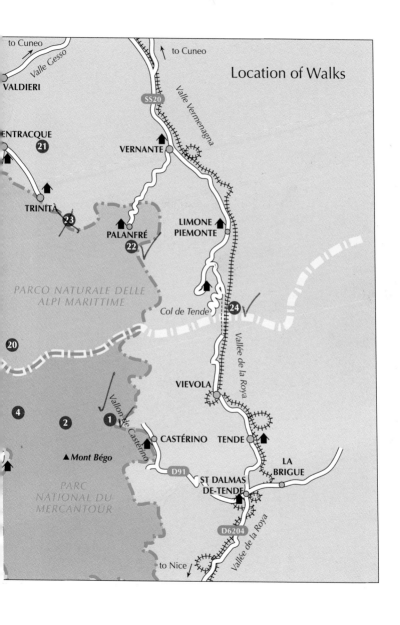

to Cuneo

VALDIERI

Valle Gesso

Valle Vermenagna

SS20

to Cuneo

Location of Walks

ENTRACQUE

21

VERNANTE

TRINITÀ

23

PALANFRÉ

22

LIMONE
PIEMONTE

PARCO NATURALE DELLE
ALPI MARITTIME

Col de Tende

24

20

Vallée de la Roya

VIEVOLA

1

Vallon de Castérino

CASTÉRINO

TENDE

LA
BRIGUE

4

2

▲ Mont Bégo

D91

ST DALMAS
DE-TENDE

PARC
NATIONAL DU
MERCANTOUR

D6204

Vallée de la Roya

to Nice

Rifugio Regina Elena at the foot of the Argentera

INTRODUCTION

THE MARITIME ALPS

As the name suggests, the Maritime Alps are related to the sea. Where the Mediterranean strays north and Italy merges into France, waves caress the sun-drenched Riviera seafront fringed with deck chairs and umbrellas. Not many holidaymakers glance away from the mesmerising sea yet, a mere 50km from those beaches, a forbidding barrier of light-grey mountains looms on the horizon. With summits soaring to over 3000m above sea level, the marvellous Maritime Alps straddle the Franco–Italian border for 190km, and form the southernmost realm of the mighty Alpine chain.

This is a region of striking contrasts. Quaint picture-book villages, crafted in stone, perch on wooded slopes in herb-scented foothills. Their dramatic backdrops of jagged rocky massifs seem to dissolve in the mists and cloud that form as warm air rises from the sea. Thick woods provide cover for wolves that flit silently through unseen, attracted by the abundance of prey – roe deer, chamois and ibex in healthy herds, the legacy of the 19th-century game reserves that were once the playground of Italy's royal family. Higher up, scores of beautiful lakes glitter like gems in cirques – the rocky bowls scooped out of the granite-schist core by the action of the vast glaciers that shrouded the region.

The Maritime Alps are shared by France and Italy, and both countries have wisely set up protected areas which work closely together. On the southern side the Parc National du Mercantour was established in 1979, France's youngest Alpine park. The name came from the summit long believed to be the highest in the range, although in fact that honour goes to the 3297m Argentera, on the northern, Italian, side. This is where the Parco Naturale delle Alpi Marittime was instituted in 1995, including within its boundaries an 1855 royal game reserve. Combined, the two parks cover an impressive 1700km^2.

For keen walkers there are an estimated 600km (373 miles) of mapped and marked pathways and the great challenge is choosing your routes from among such riches. These paths originated in ancient routes crisscrossing the Alps, trodden by prehistoric herders and later by Julius Caesar and Charlemagne. The soldiers and pilgrims tramping over the forbidding cols were joined by traders from Provence and the Mediterranean coast, on a quest for markets for salt and olive oil, and traders from landlocked Piemonte and the Po plain with wool and skins to sell.

In the 1400s, a time of especially fierce competition in commerce, a multitude of new routes were

On the path below Lac Niré (Walk 3, Stage 3)

constructed across the Maritimes, and filled with a constant stream of heavily laden mules.

Perfectly graded bridle tracks were the order of the day in the 1800s, to serve Italy's king and his hunting parties. Many were reinforced by the military during the fascist period, to serve the huge number (130!) of fortifications erected on almost every pass between the Italy and France. Half dug into mountainsides, most of these buildings are still standing. The routes in this guide visit many of these strategic cols and intriguing trails and they all have fascinating tales to tell.

The history of the border in this area is interesting in its own right. Italian unification came in 1860 and in the same year Nice and its surrounds were transferred to France in

recognition of Napoleon's support for Italy against Austria. At that time, exceptions were granted for upper swathes of the Roya, Vésubie and Tinée valleys because they were part of the Italian royal hunting reserve. But when the Italian monarchy was abolished by referendum at the close of the Second World War, the border shifted to the watershed crests, where it remains today.

WALKING

This is the first English-language guide to describe the excellent walking potential of the Maritime Alps. Good waymarking and clear maps make the region accessible to walkers of all abilities and experience and accommodation is plentiful and

At Pas Mont Colomb – a steep ascent
(Walk 3, Stage 3)

high quality. In addition to hotels, guest houses and *gîtes d'étape* on the valley floors, dozens of manned mountain huts operate throughout the summer.

The routes described here are spread across both the French and the Italian areas – 18 single-day walks and six spectacular long-distance treks which crisscross back and forth across the parks. As well as these routes, two wonderful long-distance routes pass through the Maritime Alps, both the subject of guides published by Cicerone: *The GR5 Trail. Through the French Alps: Lake Geneva to Nice* by Paddy Dillon (2008), and its mirror equivalent on the Italian side, *Through the Italian Alps: GTA* by Gillian Price (2005).

ROCK ENGRAVINGS

High in the southeastern Maritimes are tens of thousands of amazing rock engravings (or petroglyphs) – a precious heritage. Clustered around Mont Bégo, these *gravures* date back 5000 years, to the Copper and early Bronze Ages, and are believed to have held great religious significance for the tribal people who painstakingly etched them. Abstract geometric shapes, as well as stick figures ploughing or brandishing hatchets, were scratched and 'pecked' into the orange veneer of schist on cliff faces and glacially smoothed rock surfaces at the 2200m mark.

Although long known to local herders, many of whom added their own artistic contributions, the sites were not officially 'discovered' until the 1800s, principally by Clarence Bicknell, an English vicar based on the Italian Riviera. He devoted 15 years to extensive surveys, and is attributed with coining the expression 'Merveilles' to describe them. There have been more recent studies by Henry de Lumley, and at the last count the engravings totalled 35,000.

With their importance recognised and UNESCO World Heritage status assigned, they are scrupulously safeguarded under the Mercantour Park's 'Zone reglementée des Merveilles et de Fontanalba', with guards on duty round the clock to prevent a repeat of past acts of vandalism.

Individual visitors are free to visit the two main mountain sites – Fontanalba and Merveilles – but must stick to marked paths and avoid the use of metal-tipped trekking poles. Both sites are accessible from Castérino, in a branch of Vallée de la Roya. Fontanalba, with its intriguing 'Voie Sacrée', can be done in a day – see Walk 1. The same goes for the Merveilles site, but it is better visited over two days, because of the distance from the road

– see Walk 2. Authorised guided visits are held daily throughout summer – enquire at the Tende or Castérino park centres for times, costs and language options. Excursions by jeep are organised from Castérino and the Vallée de la Roya villages.

A fair number of the original petroglyphs have been shifted lock stock and barrel to a special museum at Tende; near-perfect replicas replace them in situ. The highly recommended, free-of-charge Muséé des Merveilles (☎ (33) 049 3043250, www.museedesmerveilles.com) has excellent detailed multilingual displays and masses of background information.

Rock engravings

Monte Gelàs in all its glory

The Maritime Alps are renowned for their wealth of fabulous wildflowers. From late spring through the summer months, meadows and rocky surfaces are ablaze with magnificent wine-red martagon lilies, iridescent blue gentians, rare felty edelweiss, spreads of pink alpenrose shrubs, alongside dainty orchids and lavender. Eye-catching ferns nestling under rocks are a common sight. The parsley fern, or *Criptogramma crispa*, from 'hidden' and 'curly', seeks out cool damp places. Another notable plant is a member of the daisy family; while not exceptionally beautiful, adenostyles is certainly widespread. It has clusters of lilac flowers amid large furry light-grey leaves, and grows on scree, forming carpets of silver.

Thirty endemic species stand out, restricted to the Maritime Alps but not necessarily rare. Of them, the highlight is without doubt a saxifrage, the remarkable ancient king, or *Saxifraga florulenta*. Imagine, in the harsh environment of the Alps, a cactus-like plant that spends up to 30 years clinging to a rock face 2000–3200m up, putting every ounce of energy it can muster in the short summer months to growing a fleshy rosette base in preparation for a spectacular candle-like spike bearing clusters of tiny pink blossoms. But alas, the glory is short-lived, as the flower's appearance spells rapid decline for the whole plant!

Another special is Allioni's primrose, *Primula allioni*, named after a prominent 18th-century botanist. Its pretty fuchsia-coloured blooms surrounded by small fleshy leaves can be observed in late spring clinging to limestone crannies. A little more common are two pretty endemics from the violet family: *Viola argenteria*, which sprouts on high damp scree slopes beside a type of pennycress, and the Maritime Alps pansy, *Viola valderia*, bright violet in colour and commonly found on acid rock surfaces up to 2900m.

Endemic violet

Alpenrose

Martagon lilies

Burnt orchid

Houseleek

Orange lilies

Apollo butterfly

Finally, almost as though to remind walkers of the proximity of Provence and its famous herbs, masses of aromatic plants such as thyme flourish, releasing instantly recognisable scents at the passage of a walking boot.

It's also worth visiting the well-laid-out Giardino Botanico Valderia at the Terme di Valdieri, open 15 June to 15 September, where 400 labelled species can be admired. A highly recommended companion for flower lovers is *Alpine Flowers of Britain and Europe* by C Grey-Wilson & M Blamey (Harper Collins, 1995), although at the time of writing it is out of print. (This author's own guide – *Alpine Flowers* (Cicerone) – is due out in 2011.)

WILDLIFE

Animals

According to an old saying, 'not even the wolf can eat winter', a demonstration of the deep respect people once had for the mighty **wolf** *(Canis lupus italicus)*. Notwithstanding, by the 1930s the wolf had been hunted to extinction on both sides of the Maritimes, probably for economic reasons. Rewards in 19th-century Nice were *'18F par louve pleine, 12F par loup'* (18 francs for an expectant female, 12 francs for a male). But nature takes its own course, and this reticent creature has returned, moving silently up the wild Apennine chain from Abruzzo in central Italy to re-colonise Alpine regions. The first

sightings in the Maritimes came in 1992.

Much easier for walkers to observe is the 'king of the Alps' – the **ibex** *(Capra ibex)*. In medieval times the ibex was deemed a 'walking pharmacy', as horns, blood, bones and even excrement were used to treat all manner of ailments, from poisoning to rheumatism. The ibex owes its survival to the former Italian kings who were keen hunters. To ensure exclusive game rights for their hunting parties, a series of private reserves was established in the westernmost neck of the Alps, including the Gran Paradiso in the Graians.

Twenty ibex were re-introduced to the Valdieri Game Reserve between 1920 and 1932, with great success. A proud creature, with hoofs evolved to grip well and carry it safely over incredibly steep rough mountainsides, it is almost tame, and all but ignores approaching walkers. Males have curving, 'show-off' grooved horns that can grow up to a metre long, with the length for females about half that. In preparation for adulthood, juveniles clash horns in mock battles.

Much more shy, another variety of mountain goat, the dainty **chamois** *(Rupicapra rupicapra)*, is easily recognised: it has slender 'crochet-hook' horns and white and black stripes on its face. Large herds can often be spotted grazing with their young in grassy basins, or crossing rocky slopes in single file. The young enjoy leaping

Chamoix are encountered in Vallon d'Empuonrame (Walk 3, Variant Stage 2)

and dancing on snow patches. Old males, on the other hand, live separately from a herd, often sheltering in bushes; their curious sharp whistle warns passers-by that this territory is 'taken'.

Another hoofed frequenter of high stony terrain is the **mouflon**, *Ovis ammon musimon*. A native of Corsica and Sardinia, it was introduced to the Boréon Réserve de Chasse in 1949, and has spread throughout the

19

Ibex on the dam wall in upper
Vallée de la Gordolasque
(Walk 4) and male ibex
with 'show-off' horns (below).

Mercantour, even making the occasional summer foray into Italian territory. Related to sheep, the mouflon is easily distinguished from the ibex, as its horns twist in a spiral.

The **marmot**, or 'mountain mouse', *Marmota marmota*, can be seen romping over meadows in search of succulent blooms for its largely vegetarian diet. (It's not above devouring the occasional insect.) A bit like a beaver in appearance, it lives between 1500m and 3000m in large underground colonies. A sentinel is constantly on guard for approaching eagles or foxes, and on hearing its shrill, ear-splitting whistle, young and old alike scamper down the nearest burrow to safety. Marmots hibernate through the long winter months,

when their body temperatures drop to 4–5°C; they breathe only twice a minute, and wake once a month to urinate. Now protected across the Alps, they used to be hunted for their fur and rich meat, as well as 'tamed' and paraded around towns accompanying itinerant troubadour musicians. The 'marmot oil' that is sold for the treatment of aches and pains has nothing to do with the animal, as the original balm came from the so-called marmot plum, or Briançon apricot.

Among the reptiles you might see, as well as harmless scurrying light-brown lizards, is an occasional snake. The venomous **viper**, *Vipera aspis*, prefers dry south-facing mountainsides for taking in the heat of the sun that is so essential to its

Marmot

metabolism. Greyish brown, with a diamond-like pattern along its back, it only attacks if threatened, so give it ample time to slither away, and when you are traversing overgrown areas near abandoned farms, take simple precautions such as keeping your legs covered and treading heavily. Should someone be bitten, seek medical advice as quickly as possible, and bandage and immobilise the limb. Do bear in mind that not all snakes are vipers, and not all vipers inject poison, so if there's no swelling or other adverse effects, there's probably no cause for alarm.

Birds

A delightful bird to watch out for along fast-flowing streams is the **dipper** *(Cinclus cinclus)*. With hazelnut plumage and a white neck, this agile creature flits from rock to rock before plunging into the water after worms. Noisier by far is woodland dweller the **European jay** *(Garrulus glandarius)*, whose flashy metallic-blue plumage and raucous cry warns other birds of possible danger. At much higher altitudes the cheeky **alpine chough** *(Pyrrhocorax graculus)*, with its banana-yellow beak and matching feet, is hard to miss. In great acrobatic flocks that soar to amazing heights, it swoops down to inspect picnic spots in a quest for crumbs.

A rare sight is the **wallcreeper** *(Tichodroma murari)*, usually seen in pairs. With a melodious call and telltale flash of red in its outspread wings,

it flutters against rock surfaces at surprisingly high altitudes, in search of edible insects that it captures with its slender down-turned beak.

A real treat in the skies is the lammergeier, or **bearded vulture** *(Gypaetus barbatus)*. Former inhabitant of the Maritime Alps until its extinction at the hand of man in the early 1900s, this magnificent creature is being re-introduced in pairs on a two-yearly basis on both sides of the border. With a wingspan up to 3m, adults can weigh as much as 6kg and live 20 years. They feed on animal carcasses, preferring bones, which they skilfully drop onto rocks to break into swallowable splinters. In flight the bearded vulture can be recognised by its wedge-shaped tail, distinguishable from the eagle's, which is rounded.

Over 35 pairs of the magnificent **golden eagle** *(Aquila chrysaëtos)* nest in the Maritimes. It is not unusual to see them soaring overhead on the lookout for a meal, or being subjected to aerial attacks by territorial crows. Juveniles stay with their parents at length, their feathers a much lighter creamier hue, with distinct markings.

Butterflies

Another lightweight winged creature worthy of note is the spectacular red apollo butterfly. Mainly a creamy grey colour, it has black and red 'eyes' on its wings, and a definite penchant for purple thistles.

Valleys and Bases in France

On the sparkling Côte d'Azur, the regional capital, Nice, is a logical entry point into the southern French realms of the Maritime Alps and the Mercantour Park. A convenient hotel in the centre is Nice Garden Hotel ☎ (33) 049 3873562 www.nicegarden-hotel.com.

Accessing the Alps from the west

A short distance west of the city a major road artery (N202/D6202) and *autoroute* turn north inland towards the Alps. Leave this after 25km at Plan du Var. (A railway line and the Train des Pignes come this far – get off at La Vésubie station.) Here the D2565 forks NE for the gorges of rugged Vallée de Vésubie. Some 28km up, after Lantosque and its olive groves, is the turn-off for Vallée de la Gordolasque near **Roquebillière** (tourist information and hotels). This climbs via **Belvédère** (820m), which has tourist information, shops and places to eat. Leading towards the Mont Clapier massif, it passes through the hamlet of St-Grat (1600m), where Walk 3 drops in at gîte d'étape Relais des Merveilles ☎ (33) 049 3034355, rooms with en suites as well as dormitories, open Easter to mid-October www.relaisdes-merveilles.com. The road ends at Pont du Countet (11km from Belvédère), and Walk 4 begins.

Vallée de Vésubie continues NW for a further 10km to the charming village of **St-Martin-Vésubie** (940m). Swallows nest in the overhanging timber balconies of medieval buildings. On his visit there in 1880, DW Freshfield left this lovely description: 'Amongst gaunt chestnut trunks and brown meadows, sprinkled with thousands of pale stunted crocuses, and set in a frame of pine woods, dark against the winter snow, San Martino, the Courmayeur of the Maritime Alps, came suddenly into sight.' As well as a year-round coach service from Nice, it has a camping ground 1.5km away and there's a decent choice of hotels, including Hotel La Châtaigneraie ☎ (33) 049 3032122 www.raiberti.com and Gîte La Rouguiere ☎ (33) 049 3032919 rouguiere@aol.com. There are bakeries and groceries galore, an ATM, cafés, and a gravel park where the entire population (or so it seems) engages in the serious business of playing *boules* of an afternoon. This is where Walk 3 ends. Buses go no further uphill, so the village taxi may come in handy: ☎ (33) 049 3032019.

An 8km drive higher up is **Le Boréon** (1473m). Originally named after the wild cherry trees that grow there, the name now refers to the freezing northern winter winds that blast through. It has a small dammed lake, an excellent gîte d'étape (☎ (33) 049 3032727, sleeps 40, open May to September, on reservation for the rest of the year, hot shower http://gitedu-boreon.monsite.wanadoo.fr) and two hotels: Grand Hotel Boréon ☎ (33) 049 3032035 www.hotel-boreon.com

St-Martin-Vésubie

The path to Pas des Ladres (Walks 3 and 6)

or Le Cavalet ☎ (33) 049 3032146. A special attraction is the Alpha Park (www.alpha-loup.com) where wolves can be observed in captivity. Walk 9 begins at Le Boréon. A further fork in the valley leads to the Vacherie du Boréon and the start of Walks 7 and 8, while a branch along Vallon de Salèse accesses Walks 10 and 11.

From St-Martin-Vésubie, minor road D94 forks E for the 12km to Madone de Fenestre (1903m), a renowned old sanctuary where Walks 5 and 6 start; it is also on the route of Walk 3. A manned hut provides meals and beds for walkers.

Madone de Fenestre has a fascinating history, due to its strategic position below Col de Fenestre, on a major trade route. The Romans established a staging post there, complete with a temple to Jupiter, god of the sky and thunder, to ward off deadly storms. Times and religions change, and in AD867 Benedictine monks constructed a church and hospice for passers-by on the very same spot. Unfortunately, it was sacked in the 10th century by Saracens. Reputedly angered by the infidel attack, the Virgin herself stepped in, inciting members of the crusading Templar order to rebuild the sanctuary in her name. Celebrated in colourful icons, she made a somewhat fortuitous appearance at a natural rock window (*fenêtre* in French) just to the left of the summit of Caire de la Madone. And so it was that the buildings were restored to their former glory, although fire and ransacking caused further damage over time. Nowadays, at the beginning of summer, a revered statue of the Madonna, made from cedar wood from the Holy

Tende and the railway

Land, is carried up in procession from St-Martin by the faithful; she returns to the village each winter.

Accessing the Alps from the east

Marking the easternmost edge of the Maritimes, another key valley for accessing the Mercantour is the Vallée de la Roya, which slices inland S–N with wonderful gorges. It's either a drive on the tortuous D6204, or a delightful train ride up from the Mediterranean coast (Nice or Ventimiglia), thanks to those miracles of engineering the corkscrew tunnels. (The line goes N beneath Col de Tende to Valle Vermenagna and Cuneo in Italy – see below.) Two convenient villages have railway stations: **St Dalmas-de-Tende** (696m, 76km from Nice) has shops, ATM and a monumental 'Palladio style' railway

building, a leftover from the Mussolini era. There is accommodation at B&B Le Bego ☎ (33) 049 3046532 www.sherpamerveilles.com and Hotel Le Prieuré ☎ (33) 049 3047570 www.leprieure.com. (For the second village, Tende, see below.)

Here the D91 branches NW for Val Bieugne which leads into Vallon de Castérino. The first important point is a dam 6km up, Les Mesches (1390m), 'mixing of the waters'. Here Walk 3 and the track for the Vallée des Merveilles rock engraving site begin. A further 3km on is **Castérino** (1543m). Named for a fortified medieval building, these days it comprises a cluster of small farms and hotels, including Auberge Sainte Marie-Madeleine ☎ (33) 049 3046593 www.casterino.com and *gîte d'étape*, upmarket Hotel Chamois D'Or ☎ (33) 049 3046666 www.hotelchamoisdor.net and Hotel Les Mélèzes ☎ (33) 049 3049595 www.lesmelezes.fr. This is the start for Walks 1 and 2, and can be reached by summer bus from St Dalmas and Tende.

Back in Vallée de la Roya, only 2.5km uphill from St Dalmas, is La Brigue and the access road to Notre Dame des Fontaines, an exquisitely frescoed 15th-century chapel called the 'Sistine of the Maritime Alps' ☎ (33) 049 3790934.

Not far on in the main valley is laid-back **Tende** (815m), with attractive medieval buildings and a ruined castle, not to mention a helpful tourist-cum-park information office, and the splendid Musée des Merveilles (see 'Rock engravings', pages 14–15). Accommodation (Hotel du Centre ☎

(33) 049 3046219), camping ground, restaurants, grocery shops and ATM complete the picture. Tende was visited in 1861 by the adventurous Catlow sisters, who travelled via Col de Tende: 'after passing more than fifty turns in the road we found ourselves at Tenda, a singularly picturesque town, amidst rocks, mountains, and rushing streams.' One sadly famous inhabitant was Beatrice di Tenda, whose tragic 15th-century life of violence at the hands of men inspired Bellini's opera.

Vallée de la Roya concludes at the Italian border and Col de Tende.

Valleys and Bases in Italy
The provincial capital city of Cuneo in southwest Piemonte is a convenient launching pad for excursions over the Italian flanks of the Maritime Alps.

Hotel at Sant'Anna di Valdieri

27

Only 16km SW from Cuneo, **Valdieri** (774m) is a good-sized town that hosts the headquarters of the Parco Naturale delle Alpi Marittime and an information desk. The name derives from the German for 'wood', inspired by the thickly forested surroundings. As well as a year-round bus service from Cuneo, it has grocery stores, restaurants and cafés, and an ATM, but no accommodation.

Continuing upstream in Valle Gesso (from the Celtic for 'water flowing between rocks') there is **Sant'Anna di Valdieri** (1011m), a charming village whose houses spread along the road. It can be reached by summer bus from Cuneo, and has a grocery shop, cafés, guest house/restaurant Albergo Balma Meris ☎ (39) 0171 977832 (takes credit cards), as well as B&B Ciaburna dei Ribota ☎ (39) 0171 977839 or mobile (39) 349 2915839.

The village was struck by a disastrous flood in 1810, sweeping away a shrine to St Anna, mother of Mary. Her statue miraculously came to light in a field downstream, with only a broken arm, and now occupies place of honour in the rebuilt chapel. In the mid-1800s Sant'Anna di Valdieri was the summer residence of the Savoias, the Italian royal family, which explains the smattering of elegant villas alongside traditional balconied houses. Nowadays it has only 25 permanent inhabitants. Walk 12 begins here.

Further upstream (15km from Valdieri) the road ends at the **Terme di Valdieri** (1368m), a wonderfully

restful place to stay, highly recommended by 1894 visitor WM Conway, the renowned British mountaineer and Alpine Club president: 'we took a short walk, and only then discovered the marvellous picturesque charms of the place – the walks in the woods, the view from the bridge, the hot springs in the hillside.

Lovers of natural beauty should take note of the Bagni di Valdieri.' The mineral-rich waters, from 32 springs issuing forth from the foot of Monte Matto at temperatures ranging from 26 to 69°C, are apparently beneficial for ailments of the skin and respiratory organs. It is likely that the ancient Romans appreciated the springs, though it was not until 1588 that the resort itself took shape. The present buildings date back to 1857, during the reign of King Vittorio Emanuele II, and include Swiss-inspired pavilions.

Cloaked in cool beech woods, the Terme still boasts low-key old-style spa, cafés and restaurants, a park visitor centre, excellent Alpine botanic garden and summer bus service. DW Freshfield described it as 'one of the most famous and fashionable resorts of Piedmontese society' in 1880. However he visited out of season, and the bedding offered him 'proved to contain a starved insect population' while 'the super-scriptions 'cucine', 'ristorazione', 'caffè', painted in capital letters over the doors of the corridor seemed to mock our hunger'. Comfortable accommodation nowadays is at cavernous Hotel Royal (☎ (39) 0171 97106, sleeps 178, open June – late Sept www.termedivaldieri.it), who also run the *posto tappa* for walkers (sleeps 24, open 15 June to 15 September, hot shower). Otherwise there's the family-style Hotel Turismo (☎ (39) 0171 97334, open end April to September).

Three beautiful key valleys radiate out from here: Vallone di Valasco and its waterfalls, explored in Walks 13 and 14; Vallone del Gesso della Valletta at the foot of the awesome Argentera, where Walks 15 and 16 turn up; and finally dramatic Vallone di Lourousa for Walk 17 and the continuation of Walk 9.

Not far up the valley from Valdieri a road forks S for the 6km to **Entracque** (904m), the name meaning 'between watercourses'. This pleasant old village is blessed with fountains and attractive squares where people gather to pass the time of day. It makes an excellent base for visits and is the start of Walk 21. Year-round buses connect with Cuneo, and it's also served by the summer shuttle to San Giacomo and Lago Rovina. Moreover there are good grocery shops galore, restaurants, ATM, and tourist office and park information. Accommodation is at the camping ground (see below) or hotels: Trois Etoiles ☎ (39) 0171 978283 www.hoteltroisetoiles.com or Miramonti ☎ (39) 0171 978222 www.hotelmiramontientracque.com.

A bonus are the lively summertime festivities, with traditional Occitan music and dances. On the outskirts are blocks of apartments dating back to the 1970s, when a hydro-electric plant was under construction.

Entracque

At Pas de Préfouns (Walk 11, Stage 1)

It was to become the most powerful of its kind in Italy, and an ENEL (electricity board) visitor centre is open at the foot of the Lago Piastra dam. The town is surrounded by mountains, which include a distinct limestone barrier to the NE.

The main valley splits into three key branches. Overseen by the imposing natural barrier Serrera dei Castagni is Vallone del Bousset and the hamlet of **Trinità** (1091m), with accommodation at Locanda del Sorriso (☎ (39) 0171 978388, sleeps 38, open June to September, and other times on reservation, hot shower, credit cards www.locandadelsorriso.com.) This is the start of Walk 23.

Beyond the Piastra dam the road forks again: thickly wooded Vallone di Gesso della Barra ends 9km from Entracque at the tiny hamlet of

San Giacomo (1213m). The place name, which translates as St James, is a reminder that in medieval times this was a stopover for pilgrims en route to the renowned sanctuary of Compostella in Spain. Nowadays worshippers from Entracque come this way in August during their trek to Madone de Fenestre in France. It has no shops or permanent population, but is, however, perfectly placed as the jumping-off point for Walks 19 and 20.

There is accommodation at the Park Foresteria (walkers' hostel) (☎ (39) 0171 978444, sleeps 20, open mid-June to mid-September, hot shower, cooking facilities) and the camping ground, which does meals (Sotto il Faggio, ☎ (39) 349 7305438 open June to September). There's also a park visitor centre and café-restaurant. The summer shuttle mini-bus from Entracque comes up here.

The other fork from the Piastra dam leads up steep Vallon della Rovina to Lago della Rovina (1535m), 10km from Entracque. Visitors will find a car park and snack bar at the foot of the Chiotas dam wall. Served by the summer shuttle service, it is the start of Walk 18.

From the Borgo San Dalmazzo rail and road junction on the SW outskirts of Cuneo, deep-cut Valle Vermenagna and the SS20 head S for the French border. En route it passes through **Vernante** (785m), where amenities include shops, tourist information, park visitor centre, ATM, trains and hotel accommodation at Albergo Nazionale (☎ (39) 0171 920181 www.albergonazionale. it) and its boutique twin Relais del Nazionale. The town, decorated with murals reproducing work by Attilio Mussino, renowned 1911 illustrator of the book *Pinocchio*, boasts a long tradition of hand-crafted knives with bone handles, known as *vernantin*.

A side-valley climbs 9km W to **Palanfré** (1379m), a pretty hamlet with a walkers' hostel (L'Albergh del Parco ☎ (39) 334 3052503, sleeps 30, hot shower, always open), and which is the beginning of Walk 22. Thanks to its rye crops, Palanfré once boasted a population of 300, and even its own school up until the 1960s. Credit for its rebirth goes to the farming family

Palanfré

who run the acclaimed dairy. Splendid beech woods thrive here, and there are protected specimens that are 300 years old, over 20m tall and with a diameter of 100cm.

Further S from Vernante is **Limone** (1010m). Its charming old centre is surrounded by modern flats for the high-profile ski fields above. A short bus trip away, at Panice Soprana 1400, is Hotel Tres Amis (☎ (39) 0171 928175 www.hotel3amis.it). On the ridge high above is the fascinating old pass Col de Tende (also called Colle di Tenda), visited in Walk 24. Named after the French village, for centuries it was one of the most important routes between Piemonte and the Mediterranean. In the 1500s a paved Roman road 5.2m wide was replaced by a new route, whose interminable switchbacks still snake down both sides of the pass. Nowadays the bulk of the traffic uses the more practical road and rail tunnels lower down (dating back respectively to 1882 and 1898), which burrow through to France and the Vallée de la Roya.

Col de Tende boasts some remarkable records: busiest pass on the old salt trading routes (45,000 mules transited in 1776!); first regular Alpine postal service – between Torino and Nice, beginning in 1778; and very first road tunnel through the Alps – inaugurated in 1882 after three attempts and nine years and nine months of excavations. It was also the escape route for the 15,000 refugees fleeing France during the revolution.

INFORMATION

A great deal of very useful and practical information is available about the Maritime Alps – it's just a matter of knowing where to find it. A list of relevant tourist offices and agencies follows, with websites where possible. *Syndicat d'initiative* means a tourist office in France, and *ufficio turismo* or simply *pro loco* is the equivalent in Italy.

The parks are: Parc National du Mercantour www.mercantour.eu and Parco Naturale delle Alpi Maritime www.parks.it/parco.alpi.marittime. Both have visitor centres known respectively as *maison du parc* or *casa del parco,* often doubling up as tourist information points.

Belvédère ☎ (33) 049 3035166
belvedere.si@wanadoo.fr
Castérino ☎ (33) 049 3048979
Cuneo ☎ (39) 0171 693258
www.cuneoholiday.com
Entracque ☎ (39) 0171 978616
www.entracque.org
Limone ☎ (39) 0171 925280
www.limonepiemonte.it
Nice ☎ (33) 089 2707407
www.nicetourism.com
Roquebillière ☎ (33) 049 3035160
www.roquebilliere.com
St-Martin-Vésubie ☎ (33) 049 3032128 www.vesubian.com
Tende ☎ (33) 049 3047371
www.tendemerveilles.com
Terme di Valdieri ☎ (39) 0171 97208
Valdieri ☎ (39) 0171 97397
Vernante ☎ (39) 0171 920550
pro.vernante@tiscalinet.it

At Colle della Valletta (Walk 12, Stage 2)

Useful for accommodation in France are www.guideriviera.com and www.loisirs-mercantour.com.

Guided walking tours to the Maritime Alps, with English-speaking guides, are run by Piccolo Tours www.piccolotours.com and Space Between www.space-between.co.uk.

For walkers with the time and inclination to explore more of the French region, a useful series of booklets with walking routes, *Les Guides Randoxygène*, has been published by the Conseil Général des Alpes Maritimes. They are available free at tourist offices or downloadable (*télécharger*) from www.randoxygene.org. Further interesting sites are www.balconsdumercantour.fr and www.vigilance-mercantour.fr, with postings concerning the controversial proposal for a long-distance walkers' route 'Les Balcons du Mercantour', slated for completion in 2014. The original idea proposed opening up vast unvisited realms of the Mercantour. Of the total 140km distance, about 8km of brand new paths were to be gouged out of pristine mountainsides, and several new huts constructed.

Lastly, poignant accounts of Second World War Resistance movements and refugees, along with walk itineraries. can be found at www.memoryofthealps.net.

ACCESS

By Air
Nice has the most conveniently located airport (www.nice.aeroport.fr), a short distance out of the city centre, with bus and train links. It is served by several companies from the UK, such as British Airways (www.ba.com), Ryanair (www.ryanair.com) and EasyJet (www.easyjet.com). The Vallée de Vésubie coaches stop at the airport, while for the Val di Roya railway you'll need to head for the city centre. On the Italian side of the border Torino (www.aeroportoditorino.it) has flights with BA, Ryanair and Easy Jet. City buses and trains connect with the main station Torino Porta Nuova, where frequent services leave for Cuneo (1hr 20min away). (There is also a Ryanair flight from Stansted to Cuneo but only in the ski season.)

By Road
Running south to the Mediterranean coast, toll-paying *autoroutes* from northern France and the Italian Riviera reach Nice, where local road networks take over. Cuneo is a short detour off the *autostrada* between Torino and Savona, but can be reached from eastern France by a number of minor Alpine passes.

By Rail
International trains serve both Nice and Torino. French railways SNCF run from Nice up the Vallée de la Roya to Tende and through to Cuneo. Timetables at www.ter-sncf.com/paca ☎ (33) 0891 703000.

Italian trains FS www.trenitalia.com ☎ (39) 89 2021 are useful for Torino–Cuneo as well as the Cuneo–Ventimiglia/Nice line via Valle Vermenagna, in common with SNCF.

By Bus
In France, get info and timetables from ☎ (33) 0800 060106, or at www.cg06.fr under 'Déplacements'. At the time of writing, a bargain €1 'Ticket Azur' was available on all regional bus routes. Moreover, on-demand local transport for all routes can be requested at least 24 hours ahead on the above number. For bus route n.923 (July to August only) that links Tende with St Dalmas-de-Tende and Castérino ☎ (33) 0493047371.

In Italy, contact public transport enquiries in Piemonte ☎ (39) 800 333444; Benese ☎ (39) 0171 692929 or www.benese.it serves the valleys around Cuneo, reaching Entracque, Sant'Anna di Valdieri and Terme di Valdieri. The *bus navetta del parco* midsummer shuttle service linking Entracque, San Giacomo, Lago della Rovina, Valdieri, Sant'Anna and Terme is run by GESAM ☎ (39) 0171 978616 or mobile 335 6531024. Timetables are at www.entracque.org.

WHEN TO GO

The southern bounds of the Maritime Alps can be accessible to walkers as early as May, although this will depend on levels of leftover snow from the previous winter. June is the official start of

The path heads towards L'Innominata (Walk 12, Variant Stage 2)

the *randonnée* (walking) season, and most manned huts begin operations mid-month. This coincides with the time when wildflowers explode into a riot of colour on medium-altitude meadows. North-facing cols may retain accumulated snow well into July, but generally speaking it will be soft and manageable by then. Wildlife such as ibex and chamois tend to graze valley floors until the spring meltdown gives them access to more secluded and less visible pastures higher up for their young.

On the French side, organised walking groups are common right from the word go, especially around the Vallée des Merveilles rock engraving sites, where huts can be crowded throughout the season. The Italian paths and huts tend to be relatively quiet, with the exception of summer weekends, but things warm up a lot in August, especially around the big public holiday on 15 August. Late summer and September can be idyllic, especially once school has gone back in both countries, although do be aware that the huts start closing in mid- to late September. October brings crystal-clear visibility, wonderful russet beech woods, and deserted paths. The downside is shorter days and fewer accommodation choices, but valley bases can always be used.

November to March visits will mean snowshoeing or ski touring – preferably with a local guide.

ACCOMMODATION

In the interests of sustainable tourism, both parks now apply an 'eco label' to establishments that comply with EU standards concerning energy and water saving, waste management and use of locally sourced products.

Walkers who prefer to make their base in a village and embark on day walks will be pleased to know that both sides of the border offer a selection of good-value hotels, guest houses and B&Bs. These are generally known as *auberge*, *relais* or *chambre d'hôte* in France, and *albergo*, *locanda*, *pensione* or *affittacamere* in Italy. Listings are given under 'Valleys and Bases' above.

Many French villages also feature a wonderful establishment called a *gîte d'étape*. Generally shortened to *gîte*, this is a hostel dedicated

Dorm at Rifugio Genova

to walkers. In Italy, where they are known as *posto tappa*, a couple have been opened to serve the long-distance GTA (Grande Traversata delle Alpi) route, although anyone is welcome to stay. Guests need their own sleeping sheet and towel, and accommodation is in dormitories or small rooms. A stretcher bed in a tent may be offered for overflow guests.

Bath facilities are usually shared, but the odd place has en suites. Meals are taken together at a set time with a fixed menu, in a convivial atmosphere. These hostels provide an economical alternative to hotels, and are geared to walkers' needs, doing early breakfast and picnic lunches. Booking is preferable, at least to let the guardian know how many people to expect for dinner. Expect to pay around €40 for half-board.

However, walkers embarking on the multi-day routes described in this book will be overnighting in high-altitude huts – *refuge* in French and *rifugio* in Italian. These marvellous places are inevitably set in brilliant Alpine landscapes, far from roads and mod cons, and allow walkers to enjoy the mountains without being weighed down by camping gear. Just a lightweight sleeping sheet and towel need be carried – blankets are always plentiful.

The refuges provide a multi-course evening meal and breakfast, bunk bed accommodation and shared bathroom facilities – more often than not quite spartan. Meals in French

Castérino accommodation

huts follow a set menu, while some in Italy allow for individual orders. The majority of the huts are owned by the Alpine clubs of France (CAF – Club Alpin Français) and Italy (CAI – Club Alpino Italiano). Facilities are open to everyone and discounted rates are available for members, and for members of clubs with reciprocal agreements.

Residents in Great Britain can join the UK branch of the Austrian Alpine Club www.aacuk.uk.com ☎ (44) 01707 386740 or the British Mountaineering Council www. thebmc.co.uk ☎ (44) 0870 0104878.

In terms of organisation, the French huts tend to be a little more regimented than their Italian equivalents, but both observe 'lights out' and silence from 10pm to 6am. Guests leave boots and cumbersome

equipment downstairs and don slippers or sandals inside.

Demi pension or *mezza pensione*, at the cost of €30–36 at the time of writing, includes a cooked evening meal, bed and breakfast. In France, dinner is a soup, main course of meat with a veg and carbohydrate (rice, pasta or potatoes), then cheese and/or dessert. They'll usually whip up an omelette for vegetarians if you ask. Italian dinner starts with pasta or soup, moves on to meat, and concludes with dessert. Drinks are charged extra in both cases. Breakfast is continental – bread, butter and jam washed down with milky coffee (*cafè au lait/caffè latte*), tea, or hot *chocolat* in France.

Lunch is usually available at huts. In France this tends to be limited to a snack or omelette, whereas the

37

Italians go the whole hog, with pasta, soup, meat and more. In contrast, packed picnic lunches are limited to a roll with cheese (*panino con formaggio*), ham (*prosciutto*) or salami in Italy, while the French do themselves proud, with a serving of cold pasta or couscous, cheese, biscuits, chocolate, fruit and a drink, if not a *sandwich au fromage* or *au jambon* (cheese or ham sandwich). Place your order for *picnique* or *pranzo al sacco* the previous evening.

Concerning reservations, on the Italian side advance booking is only usually necessary for weekends in midsummer. The French side tends to be a little busier due to organised trekking groups, although two people can usually be squeezed into a dorm at the last minute. A handy system of internet booking has been activated for the CAF huts Cougourde, Madone de Fenestre, Nice, Valmasque and Merveilles at www.cafresa.org. You can book several months ahead and see online how many vacancies there are.

Note Several important French huts have no telephone so the **only** way to book is over the internet and Refuge des Merveilles (which does) is in great demand – be warned!

Opening periods for the huts are given at the end of the relevant walks. However, inclement weather often means changes, so take the dates with a pinch of salt and always check at the start and end of the season.

On both sides of the border it's a good idea to ask hut staff to phone

and reserve ahead for your intended destinations. Contact details are given under relevant walks. However, while all the Italian huts have phones, several on the French side don't.

Note Phone numbers are listed with international country codes in brackets. Remember that Italian numbers **always** require the initial 0, even when the call is made from within the country. Exceptions are Italian mobile numbers (which start with 3) and emergency calls to 118 and the like. For calls inside France the 0 needs removing; French mobiles are recognisable for their initial 06.

CAMPING

Many French trekkers carry their own food and gear, preferring to bivouac (sleep out). As long as campers are at least 1hr from a road this is allowed in the Mercantour, but only between 7pm and 9am. (The time limit is relaxed on rainy days.) Wild pitches are strictly forbidden in the special Merveilles-Fontanalba rock engraving area, with the sole exception of the immediate vicinity of a manned refuge.

Many French huts actually have a specially designated area for tents – *always* check with staff before setting up camp. On the Italian side *bivaccare* (or wild camping) is allowed for two successive nights in one location; if you shift to a different valley, two more nights are permitted. There are also a couple of unmanned huts

Descending from Colle del Brocan (Walk 12, Stage 4)

passed on these routes – Bivacco Moncalieri (Walks 12 and 19) and Bivacco Guiglia (Walks 11 and 14). They mean a roof over your head, a bunk bed and a water supply nearby but little else.

Well-equipped camping grounds can be found in most valleys, including the following.

- Entracque: Campeggio Valle Gesso ☎ (39) 0171 978247 www.campingvallegesso.com
- St-Martin-Vésubie: Les Champouns ☎ (33) 049 3032372 http://champouns. romsoft-s.com
- San Giacomo: Sotto il Faggio ☎ mobile (39) 349 7305438 open June to September
- Tende: Saint Jacques ☎ (33) 049 3047608 open 1 May to 30 September

DOS AND DON'TS

- Don't set out late on walks, and always have extra time up your sleeve to allow for detours because of collapsed bridges, wrong turns and missing signposts. Plan on getting to your destination at an early hour; this is of special importance on the French side – its proximity to the Mediterranean coast means that in summer masses of warm, moisture-laden air move inland quickly and collide with the mountain barrier, so afternoon storms are common.
- Find time to get in good shape before setting out on your holiday, as it will maximise enjoyment. The wonderful scenery will be better appreciated in the absence of exhaustion, and healthy walkers will react better in an emergency.

Lago Bianco del Gelàs from Passo dei Ghiacciai (Walk 12, Stage 6)

- Don't be overly ambitious. Choose itineraries suited to your capability, and read the walk description before setting out.
- Stick with your companions and don't lose sight of them. Remember that groups progress at the pace of the slowest member.
- Avoid walking in brand-new boots, as they may well cause blisters, but leave those worn-out old boots in the shed, as they may be unsafe on slippery terrain. Choose your footwear carefully!
- Don't overload your rucksack. Weigh it on the bathroom scales – 10kg is the absolute maximum for multi-day walking! Drinking water and food mean extra weight. Finally, bear in mind that as the afternoon wears on and that hut seems ever further away, your pack will inexplicably get heavier.
- Check the weather forecast if possible – tourist offices and hut guardians are in the know. The weather forecast (*météo*) for France is ☎ (33) 0892680206 http://france.meteofrance.com and in Italy the *meteo* is at www.arpa.piemonte.it. Never set out on a long route if conditions are bad. Even a broad track can become treacherous in adverse weather, and high-altitude terrain enveloped in thick mist makes orientation difficult. An altimeter is useful – if at a known altitude (such as that of a refuge) your altitude reading is too high, this means that the atmospheric pressure has dropped and the weather could change for the worse.
- Carry any rubbish back to the valley where it can be disposed of

View to Valrossa from upper Valasco (Walk 13)

correctly; don't expect hut staff to deal with it. Even organic waste such as apple cores and orange peel is best not left lying around, as it upsets the diet of animals and birds.

- Be considerate when making a toilet stop. Keep away from watercourses, don't leave unsightly paper lying around, and remember that abandoned huts and rock overhangs could serve as life-saving shelter for someone else!
- Wildlife should not be disturbed or handled, tempting though it may be at times, and dogs should never be taken into these mountains. Collecting flowers, insects or minerals is forbidden.
- Fires are strictly forbidden.
- Carry extra protective clothing as well as energy foods for emergency situations. Remember that in normal circumstances the temperature drops an average of 6°C for every 1000m you climb.
- Learn the international rescue signals – see 'Emergencies' below. **DO NOT** rely on your mobile phone, as there may be no signal. In electrical storms, don't shelter under trees or rock overhangs, and keep away from metallic fixtures.
- Lastly, don't leave your common sense at home.

WHAT TO TAKE

The choice of gear can make or break a walking holiday. It's worth spending time beforehand on careful preparation. The following checklist may be helpful.

- Comfortable lightweight rucksack with waist straps; plastic bags or stuff bags for separating contents.
- Walking boots with ankle support and non-slip soles, preferably not brand new.
- Light footwear such as sandals for evenings.
- Lightweight sleeping sheet or bag liner, essential for overnight stays in mountain huts.
- Small towel and personal toiletries in small containers.
- First aid kit and essential medicines.
- Sunglasses, hat, lip salve and high factor suncream. For every 1000m you climb the intensity of the sun's UV rays increases by ten per cent, augmented by reflection on snow. This, combined with lower levels of humidity and pollution, which act as filters in other places, mean you need a cream with a much higher protection factor than at sea level.
- Rainproof gear – either an anorak, over-trousers and rucksack cover, or a large poncho. Walkers who wear spectacles will appreciate a folding umbrella, though it won't be much use in a high wind.

- Telescopic trekking poles, to distribute rucksack weight over the body and off wonky knees, will provide psychological support during steep descents and stream crossings, keep sheep dogs at bay and even double as washing lines.
- Layers of clothing for dealing with everything from scorching sun to a snow storm: T-shirts and shorts, comfortable long trousers (not jeans), warm fleece and a windproof jacket and a woolly hat and gloves for emergencies.
- A supply of high-energy food, such as muesli bars and chocolate.
- Maps, altimeter, compass and binoculars.
- Camera and film or memory cards, and battery charger with adaptor for digitals.
- Whistle, small headlamp or torch with spare batteries, for calling for help.
- Supply of euros in cash and a credit card. ATMs can be found at most of the towns encountered. Assume that gîtes d'étape and huts don't accept credit cards unless otherwise stated.
- Salt tablets or electrolyte powders to combat salt depletion caused by excessive sweating.
- Water bottle – plastic mineral water bottles are perfect.
- Mobile phone, charger and adaptor.

MAPS

Excellent maps are available for both sides of the Maritime Alps. They are widely available at local outlets, as well as leading map stores and out-door suppliers in the UK.

The sections of the Mercantour Park in France covered in this guide need the 1:25,000 series by IGN (www.ign.fr), *carte de randonnée* sheets 3841OT Vallée de la Roya and 3741OT Vallée de la Vésubie. The only

Signpost in France

Signpost in Italy

drawback is that where they stray even metres into Italian territory, the map converts to different graphics and paths all but disappear. The Mercantour uses a brilliant system whereby the numbers on marker poles at key junctions are found on the maps, so you always know exactly where you are. These are referred to in the walk descriptions and denoted by a 'P' and then two or three digits, eg '123' (so 'P123').

For Italy a single map is sufficient – Cartoguida 1 Parco Naturale delle Alpi Marittime 1:25,000 by Blu Edizioni (www.bluedizioni.it), with a clear design that makes it especially easy to read. The sole exception is Walk 24, which needs the first French map.

A last but not least suggestion is to purchase the handy 1:50,000 maps Montagnes sans Frontière, published by L'Arciere, Cuneo, 1995. Designed to accompany the guidebook of the same name in Italian and French describing trans-frontier routes, they are also sold as a set for a reasonable €8. Not completely up to date, but worthwhile for an overview.

EMERGENCIES

For medical matters, walkers who live in the EU need a European Health Insurance Card (EHIC), which has replaced the old E111. Holders are entitled to free or subsidised emergency health treatment in both France and Italy. UK residents can apply online at www.dh.gov.uk. Travel insurance to cover an Alpine walking holiday is also strongly recommended, as the cost of rescue can be hefty. Alpine club members are usually covered by a special policy (see 'Accommodation').

'Help' is *au secours!* in French (pronounced *oh secore*) and *aiuto!* in Italian (pronounced *eye-yoo-toh*). Experienced staff at refuges can always be relied on in emergencies.

The international rescue signals can come in handy: the call for help is **six** signals per minute. These can be visual (such as waving a handkerchief or flashing a torch) or audible (whistling or shouting). They are to be repeated after a one-minute pause. The answer is **three** visual or audible

Both arms raised
- help needed
- land here
- YES (to pilot's questions)

One arm raised diagonally, one arm down diagonally
- help not needed
- do not land here
- NO (to pilot's questions)

Bivacco Guiglia and its amazing view to the Argentera

signals per minute, to be repeated after a one-minute pause. Anyone who sees or hears such a call for help must contact the nearest refuge, police station or the like as quickly as possible.

In France the general emergency telephone number is ☎ 112, an ambulance (*samu*) ☎ 15, and the police (*gendarmerie*) ☎ 17. Mountain rescue (*secours en montagne*) for the Mercantour is ☎ (33) 049 7222222.

In Italy the general emergency telephone number is ☎ 113, while calls for *soccorso alpino* (mountain rescue) need to be made to ☎ 118.

The arm signals shown in the box (facing page) could be useful for communicating with a helicopter:

USING THIS GUIDE

All of the walk descriptions in this guide begin with headings listing the following essential information, for both single and multi-day routes.

Walking Time This does not include pauses for picnics, admiring views, taking photos and 'nature stops', so always add on a good couple of hours to be realistic. **Note** In the description for short walks, partial timing is given in brackets at useful landmarks.

Difficulty On a scale of 1–3 as follows:

- *Grade 1* refers to a fairly straightforward route on easy terrain with no special difficulty; such itineraries are good walks for beginners.

- *Grade 2* is suitable for reasonably fit walkers with minimum mountain experience.
- *Grade 3* routes may entail exposed passages and/or orientation problems and can rate 'tough'.

That said, everyone should bear in mind that adverse weather such as mist and low visibility, strong wind or rain, can increase difficulty, making even a Grade 1 path downright dangerous at times.

Distance An approximate measure of walk or stage length, this is given in both kilometres and miles.

Ascent/Descent While apparently of little interest to hill walkers, in the Alps it is of utmost importance, much more so than distance. Taken in relation to timing it is an indication of how strenuous a route is. For instance a height gain or ascent of 300m in 1hr is fairly leisurely, whereas 600m in the same time means you can expect to be puffing up a pretty steep slope. On moderately steep terrain, it takes 1hr on average to ascend 300m (approximately 1000ft) or descend 500m.

During the walk descriptions, 'path' is used to mean a narrow pedestrian-only way, 'track' and 'lane' are unsurfaced but vehicle-width, and 'road' is sealed and open to traffic unless specified otherwise. Compass bearings are in abbreviated form (N, S, NNW and so on) as are right (R) and left (L). Useful landmarks encountered en route are in bold type; altitudes are in metres, given as 'm' (100m = 328ft).

Incredibly vast views en route to Colle del Brocan (Walk 12, Stage 4)

WALK 1
Fontanalba Rock Engravings Circuit

Walking Time	4hr 30min or 1 day
Difficulty	Grade 1–2
Distance	17km/10.5 miles
Ascent/Descent	700m/700m
Start/Finish	Castérino
Access	From St Dalmas-de-Tende in Vallée de la Roya, the D91 climbs NE into the Vallon de Castérino. A midsummer bus from Tende via St Dalmas-de-Tende runs up to the settlement of Castérino.

A beautiful circuit in the southeastern Maritime Alps, leading through forest and across thickly flowered slopes to elevated glacial cirques, where there is magnificent Alpine scenery and a clutch of very pretty lakes to be enjoyed. However, Vallon de Fontanalba is synonymous with the remarkable mountainside rock engravings carved by prehistoric man 5000 years ago; they have made this part of the Mercantour famous. The walk destination is the *pièce de résistance*, the so-called 'Voie Sacrée' – a 50m long, inclined slab of schist, polished to a sheen by the passage of long-gone ice masses. Highlighted by the thin orange-red veneer, a total of 284 petroglyph figures have been discovered on this open-air drawing board. Guided walks are organised during summer. (See 'Rock Engravings', pages 14–15.)

Quiet Castérino, where the walk starts, offers a number of hotels and restaurants and a gîte, as well as an informative park visitor centre. Refuge de Fontanalba, encountered during the walk, is an alternative place to stay.

The walk can be shortened marginally by driving as far as the 1719m turn-off (P395), and returning there afterwards instead of descending to Castérino. This will save about 1hr.

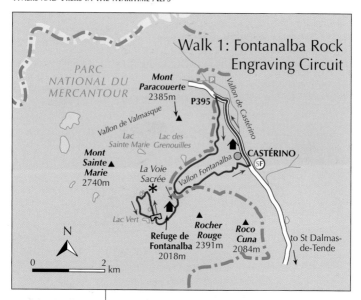

Walk 1: Fontanalba Rock Engraving Circuit

WALK

From **Castérino** (1543m) walk NNW up the narrow road for 3km to the car park and turn-off at 1719m (P395, 45min). Fork L through the shady larch wood on a bumpy old military track. It climbs steadily SSE high over Vallon de Fontanalba, emerging in flowery meadows. Ignore the fork R at 1969m, unless you have time for the short detour to Lacs des Grenouilles (though don't expect to see any frogs). ◄ A stream is crossed to a hut and junction (P390) for the fork R to **Refuge de Fontanalba** (2018m, 1hr 15min), a simple but welcoming establishment.

> On this stretch rewards come in the form of views onto a cirque of light-grey rock spattered with snow, and closed off by a forbidding rock barrier that includes Mont Bégo SW.

Stay on the rough jeep track for the climb SW past aged larch trees and waterfalls to a **bridge** and turn-off (2130m, 20min) for the important rock engravings site. Keep R (N) up the track, which doubles as a good lookout over the Castérino valley. Ignore turn-offs L. After two huts are signs for 'La Voie Sacrée'. A path leads to the base of the polished rock slabs covered with stick figures and geometric shapes. Helpful charts indicate key groupings.

At the top of the steps is a belvedere with an instructive *table d'orientation* naming all the mountains visible, including far-off Marguareis, NE in the Ligurian Alps. Drop to a hut then fork R to skirt the pretty **Lacs Jumeaux** ('twin lakes', 2222m). The path descends S past marmot burrows into an attractive peat basin, bright yellow with marsh marigolds, where there are tinkling streams and gnarled larch trees stand as sentinels. ▶

With a little patience shy chamois may be spotted on the surrounding mountainsides.

An outcrop is rounded and beautiful **Lac Vert**, trimmed with conifers (2188m), soon reached. The lake's water reflects elegant Cime de Chanvrairée. Through banks of alpenrose the path returns to the **bridge** (1hr) and main track. Retrace your steps via **Refuge de Fontanalba** (2018m, 20min) to the P390 junction and turn R (SE). This 4WD track follows the southern edge of Vallon de Fontanalba through beautiful conifer forest thick with wildflowers. Surprisingly steep hairpin bends lead down to the road at **Castérino** (1543m, 50min), close to the *maison du park* information point.

Refuge de Fontanalba ☎ (33) 049 3048919, sleeps 25, solar-heated shower, open 14 June to 15 September. Owned by Nice Ski Club, it does not offer reciprocal reductions for Alpine Club members.

Castérino
Auberge Sainte Marie-Madeleine ☎ (33) 049 3046593 www.casterino.com, including gîte. Hotel Chamois D'Or ☎ (33) 049 3046666 www.hotel chamoisdor.net Hotel Les Mélèzes ☎ (33) 049 3049595 www.lesmelezes.fr

Lacs Jumeaux

The fascinating Voie Sacrée

WALK 2
Mont Bégo Loop

Walking Time	12hr or 3 days
Difficulty	Grade 2
Distance	25km/15.4 miles
Ascent/Descent	1372m/1372m
Start/Finish	Castérino
Access	From St Dalmas-de-Tende in Vallée de la Roya, the D91 climbs NE into the Vallon de Castérino. A midsummer bus from Tende via St Dalmas-de-Tende runs up to Castérino.

This particularly exciting route passes through spectacular glacially shaped landscapes, with photogenic lakes crowned with jagged mountains at every turn of the path. Walkers spend time in beautiful woods as well as traversing two high cols. The circuit also takes in the renowned Merveilles rock engravings clustered around Mont Bégo, a bulky mountain that peaks at 2872m. More information about the site can be found in 'Rock Engravings' on pages 14–15.

A glance at the place names here suggests a fearsome reputation for the valley: there's Devil's Peak (Cime du Diable) and Hell Valley (Val d'Enfer) – perhaps references to violent summer storms? For centuries the Vallée des Merveilles area was used by keepers of livestock, and its earliest known name was *arpi* ('pasture'). (The current name – Vallée des Merveilles – was not coined until the 1900s, once the importance of the petroglyphs was appreciated.) In the Middle Ages there was intense rivalry in Vallée de la Roya, between the shepherds of Tende and the goatherds of Saorge, so the authorities made them take turns – three years grazing for sheep versus one for goats. Nowadays the grass is shared by four flocks in all – a total of 1500 animals.

On the walk, three welcoming mountain refuges are encountered. Refuge des Merveilles is best booked in

PARCO NATURALE DELLE
ALPI MARITTIME

Walk 2:
Mont Bégo Loop

Lac de l'Agnel

PARC
NATIONAL DU
MERCANTOUR

Refuge de
Valmasque
2221m

Mont
Paracouerte
2385m

P

Vallon de Castérino

Lac Vert

Vallon de Valmasque

Lac Noir

Lac Sainte Marie   Lac des
Grenouilles

Vallon Fontanalba

CASTÉRINO
SF

Mont
Ste-Marie
2740m

Lac du Basto

Mont du
Grand
Capelet
2935m

P95

Lac de
Ste Marie

Refuge de
Fontanalba
2018m

Lac Vert de
Fontanalba

Rocher
Rouge
2391m

Roco
Cuna
2084m

Baisse de
Valmasque

Baisse de
Vallauretta

LES
MESCHES

Mont
Bégo
2872m

Vallée des Merveilles

Vallon de la Minière

P383

to
St Dalmas-
de-Tende

Lac Long
Superiore

Refuge des
Merveilles
2130m

N

0   2
└────────────────┘ km

advance, in view of the high visitor numbers here. Also,
be aware that snow cover around Baisse de Valmasque
may be heavy at the start of the summer, but rest assured
that you will not be alone.

Car owners may prefer to park at the P395 turn-off, 3km from Castérino, and follow Walk 1 to Refuge de Fontanalba. At trek's end, vehicles are easily collected here.

Alternative access to this circuit is also possible by starting out from Les Mesches on the road to Castérino. A short walk away is the recommended gîte d'étape, Neige et Merveilles, in a converted mining village. The way climbs to Refuge des Merveilles, thus cutting out Vallon de Fontanalba – see Walk 3.

STAGE 1

Castérino to Refuge des Merveilles

Walking Time	5hr 15min
Difficulty	Grade 2
Distance	9.6km/5.9 miles
Ascent/Descent	947m/360m

A lengthy but problem-free opener, this stage heads up the Fontanalba valley and slips across a pass. After a modest descent, a second long uphill section via waterfalls ends in the wonderful cirque beneath Mont Bégo.

At **Castérino** (1543m), a matter of metres downhill from the *maison du parc*, turn up at P391 for the rough track W. This wastes no time gaining height on steep hairpin bends through thick conifer forest. Masses of colourful wildflowers brighten the undergrowth as you head up Vallon de Fontanalba. Ignore the side-tracks used by woodcutters, and proceed to the hut and junction (1943m, P390). Here turn L uphill in common with Walk 1 for the short distance to

1hr 45min – Refuge de Fontanalba (2018m) set in cool forest. ☎ (33) 049 3048919, sleeps 25, solar-heated

53

shower, open 14 June to 15 September. Owned by Nice Ski Club, it does not offer reciprocal reductions for Alpine Club members.

The recommended circuit requires at least 1hr extra – see Walk 1 for the description.

A path cuts through trees to rejoin the rough jeep track SW. Not far up is the turn-off (P387, 2130m) for the Fontanalba rock engravings. ◄

A track of military origin continues uphill W to fork P386, where you veer L (ESE). A path makes its way towards the rocky crest that separates the Fontanalba and Minière valleys.

1hr – Baisse de Vallauretta (2270m, P385) and its long-abandoned barracks are easily reached, with Cime de Chanvrairée towering alongside. Views back over the lakes are inspirational, with Mont Bégo at the western extremity of the ridge. A well-trodden path now begins a lengthy descent S across the initially bare flanks of Vallon de la Minière, the name a reference to the former mining community at Valaura, far below. It swings SE to drop

Refuge des Merveilles

past the old shepherds huts of Gias Valauretta and enters light woodland. After a stretch due E you join the main valley path at **P383** (1hr, 1682m). Turn sharp R over side-streams to the wooden bridge across the river.

Amidst luxuriant vegetation and masses of bilberry shrubs, the path now climbs SW to join the *piste* from Les Mesches. However, a signed *sentier* soon branches R for a gorgeous stretch alongside waterfalls, in a magnificent setting of rock that has been rounded and smoothed by glaciers. The climb concludes on the lip of a basin where you pick up the piste once more. In the company of Mont Bégo, jagged Cime des Lacs and Cime du Grand Capelet appear. A rock-strewn amphitheatre is traversed to reach marvellous Lac Long Superiore, on whose banks perches

1hr 30min – Refuge des Merveilles (2130m). ☎ (33) 049 3046464 CAF, sleeps 79, open 17 June to 28 September. This well-run hut has vast dormitories, satisfying multi-course dinners, but only a cold shower. A very popular establishment, it even attracts chamois, which graze on the adjoining slopes in the evening.

STAGE 2
Refuge des Merveilles to Refuge de Valmasque

Walking Time	4hr 15min
Difficulty	Grade 2
Distance	7.9km/4.9 miles
Ascent/Descent	425m/334m

An outstanding day's walking, whose highlights include the prehistoric rock engravings, then a spectacular pass and a string of beautiful vast lakes.

Leave **Refuge des Merveilles** (2130m) and head W, following the GR52 red/white paint splashes along the

One especially curious site is a cliff face covered with graffiti – old and not-so-old – left by soldiers, priests and even a local bandit.

pretty lakeside. The gradient is gentle, on a paved way through alpenrose and marmot territory. Ignore the fork L (P93) for Pas de l'Arpette and bear R (N) on the earth path, climbing above Lac Long Superiore, approaching Vallée des Merveilles at last, in the shade of Mont Bégo. It's not far at all to the first of the prehistoric petroglyphs, easily identifiable, as all have explanatory signs. ◄

A gushing mountain stream accompanies the path via terraces occupied by peat bogs – it all certainly lives up to its marvellous name! Not until the last lake is passed at 2383m in the shadow of Mont du Grand Capelet does the path begin serious ascent, zigzags taking the sting out of the steepness.

2hr – Baisse de Valmasque (2549m) is a simply breathtaking spot with magnificent views over Lac du Basto, surmounted by jagged light-grey peaks spattered with snow.

At Baisse de Valmasque with Lac du Basto

The downward route bears briefly R on a good winding path that moves to the centre of this broad open valley. Some snow cover can be expected early in the season, so

Refuge de Valmasque on Lac Vert

keep an eye out for markings. Across rock/earth terrain you pass P95 (30min, the fork L for Baisse du Basto) and approach the water's edge, dominated by the imposing Rochers de Ste-Marie crest (E). Over chattering streams, the paved path, marked with green/cream, follows the R bank of beautiful Lac du Basto and drops past a dam wall.

Next is ominous-sounding Lac Noir, surveyed by ibex on high perches. Over the rock barrier at the end, lovely Lac Vert stretches out, including an inspiring view of the refuge on its rock promontory. Down close to the shore, P97 indicates a tricky scramble to the hut, but it's more straightforward (if a little longer) to continue down the rock corridor to the P98 fork (1hr 15min), where you turn L for the final 15min to

2hr 15min – Refuge de Valmasque (2221m), a great place to enjoy a drink on the wonderful terrace, or stay

57

Lovely waterfalls are encountered during the descent

the night. CAF, sleeps 52, open 1 June to 30 September, occasional weekends May and Oct, cold shower. (**Note** The refuge has no telephone.)

If you do not intend to sleep here, ignore the detour to the hut and continue towards Castérino, saving 30min.

STAGE 3
Refuge de Valmasque to Castérino

Walking Time	2hr 30min
Difficulty	Grade 2
Distance	7.5km/4.6 miles
Descent	678m

This undemanding descent skirts an awesome glacially formed cliff, then proceeds through pretty woodland alive with wildlife, to conclude in the hospitable hamlet of Castérino.

From **Refuge de Valmasque** (2221m) the path returns to the P98 fork and descends easily in knee-friendly zigzags to two magnificent waterfalls beneath Mont Ste-Marie. Through pretty larch and alpenrose cover, where chamois graze, you continue NE downhill alongside the severe rock barrier that supports Lac Vert. An old military road is joined (P374, 1hr) in this wonderfully green valley, which soon narrows, the river flowing through a mere slit far below.

2hr – car park (1719m) marks the start of a minor surfaced road. Making the most of the odd short-cut, it's not far at all back to

30min – Castérino (1543m). Accommodation is listed under Walk 1.

WALK 3
Vallée de la Roya to Vallée de Vésubie

Walking Time	18hr 30min or 5 days
Difficulty	Grade 2–3
Distance	38km/23.4 miles
Ascent/Descent	2372m/2822m
Start/Finish	Les Mesches/St-Martin-Vésubie
Access	From St Dalmas-de-Tende in Vallée de la Roya, the D91 climbs NE into Vallon de Castérino. There is a midsummer bus from St Dalmas and Tende that will drop you at Les Mesches. (Otherwise, on foot with signed short-cuts, allow 2hr for the 6km with 680m height gain.) At walk's end, St-Martin-Vésubie has year-round buses south to Nice.

This extended trek is a memorable way to visit the spectacular heart of the Mercantour National Park, spending five breathtaking days on high paths with a kaleidoscope of scenery. The traverse leads east–west, connecting transport artery Vallée de la Roya on the easternmost margin of the Maritime Alps with centrally placed Vallée de Vésubie. En route it takes in the renowned Vallée des Merveilles rock engraving site, full of prehistoric mystery (see 'Rock Engravings' in the Introduction, pages 14–15), a couple of high arduous passes, and some beautifully placed refuges, before finally descending in stages to end at a charming French village.

The two central sections – Stages 2 and 3 – involve especially demanding traverses via the dizzy passages Baisse du Basto and Pas Mont Colomb, encountering terrain of an especially steep and unstable nature. However, they can be avoided by using the slightly lower crossings Pas de l'Arpette and Baisse de Prals, and touching on the middle part of Vallée de la Gordolasque, with a conveniently placed gîte d'étape – see Variant Stage 2 and Variant Stage 3.

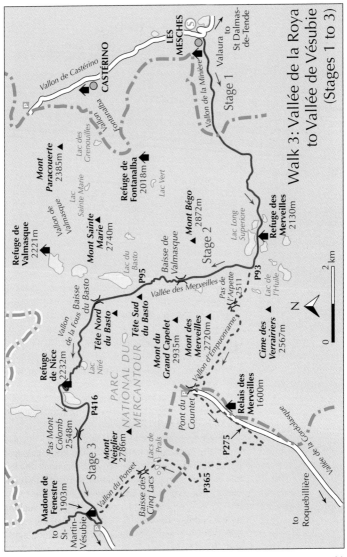

Walk 3: Vallée de la Roya
to Vallée de Vésubie
(Stages 1 to 3)

STAGE 1
Les Mesches to Refuge des Merveilles

Walking Time	2hr 30min
Difficulty	Grade 2
Distance	6.8km/4.2 miles
Ascent	740m

An easy if constantly uphill route via the former mining village of Valaura, part of which has been beautifully renovated as an excellent gîte d'étape. Valaura was a leading silver and zinc mine in the 18th and 19th centuries. There is pretty woodland with waterfalls along the route for the rest of the way to the lakeside location of Refuge des Merveilles, in the shade of legendary Mont Bégo.

Above the dammed lake and electricity substation at **Les Mesches** (1390m), at P84, a marked concrete-base lane leads due W. Entering Vallon de la Minière, it soon reaches

15min – Valaura (1500m), the old mining village. At P85 fork R, leaving the 4WD track (which does proceed to Refuge des Merveilles, but takes longer and isn't as pretty). Unless you plan to stay over, ignore 'Accueil' ('reception') and bear L to pass the old Italian barracks, now comfortable lodgings. **Gîte d'étape Neige et Merveilles** ☎ (33) 049 3046240 sleeps 150, open mid-February to mid-November, hot shower, www.neige-merveilles.com.

A narrow lane climbs steeply W around a rock outcrop and huts. The gradient eases a little as you pass a small lake, then follow the gently cascading stream through pasture thick with spectacular swathes of flowers, including orange lilies and mountain lavender. ◄ Further on a path takes over and, joined by the route from the Fontanalba valley (Walk 2), crosses the river amidst larch trees and bilberry shrubs.

In the distance WNW looms Mont Bégo, beyond rock barriers colonised by pine trees.

62

Vallon de la Minière

The 4WD track (*piste*) is joined at P89a, but soon abandoned for an especially enjoyable path marked 'Sentier', a wonderful climb beside waterfalls in a magnificent setting. On the lip of a vast amphitheatre basin, scattered with *roches mountonnées* left by a glacier, the piste is rejoined for level walking. The jagged peaks of Cime du Lac and Mont du Grand Capelet can be seen, and not far ahead on the L bank of expansive Lac Long supérieur stands

2hr 15min – Refuge des Merveilles (2130m). ☎ (33) 049 3046464 CAF, sleeps 79, open 17 June to 28 September, cold shower. An efficiently run hut with large dorms and satisfying dinners. Book well ahead, as it is very popular; it even attracts chamois, which graze on the adjoining slopes in the evening.

STAGE 2
Refuge des Merveilles to Refuge de Nice

Walking Time	6hr
Difficulty	Grade 3
Distance	8.8km/5.4 miles
Ascent/Descent	712m/610m

First of all this stage visits the remarkable concentration of old rock engravings in aptly named Vallée des Merveilles (remember that this is a special reserve, and walkers should refrain from using metal-tipped trekking poles and from leaving marked paths). Then two high passes are crossed – the second involves tricky terrain where an expert foot is needed, as well as good weather and clear visibility. Snow typically lies late on the northern faces and can be icy in low temperatures. A plunge down a valley glittering with lakes finishes at strategically placed Refuge de Nice.

Leave **Refuge des Merveilles** (2130m) following red/white waymarks for the GR52, heading due W above the lake and through a pretty landscape of rock, larch and alpenrose, enlivened by chamois and marmots. In the early morning Mont Bégo throws its vast shadow over the path. At **P93** (15min) fork R (N) on the earth path. This passes high above the W shore of Lac Long supérieur, approaching Vallée des Merveilles at last. The first of the prehistoric petroglyphs is soon reached – easily located thanks to clear explanatory signs. ◄

A curious cliff site is covered with graffiti – old and not-so-old – left by soldiers, priests and even a bandit.

A gushing stream accompanies the path via terraces occupied by peat bogs, and a scattering of lakes, possibly snowbound in early summer. Not until the last lake is passed, at 2383m in the shadow of Mont du Grand Capelet, does the path begin a serious ascent, countless zigzags taking the sting out of the steepness to

2hr – Baisse de Valmasque (2549m), a simply breathtaking spot with a magnificent view over Lac du Basto and its crown of jagged light-grey peaks.

Keep R to embark on a good winding path N that soon moves down the centre of this broad open valley. ▸ Navigating around boulders and across scree/earth terrain, you reach the **P95 junction** (30min, 2400m).

Ignore the route straight ahead for Refuge de Valmasque, and instead fork L (NW), staying with the GR52. Climbing gently at first, the traverse cuts across the middle of Tête Sud du Basto, and passes along a broad corridor with spectacular views over Lac du Basto. A mini lake lies beneath Tête Nord du Basto in a vast rockscape, leading to a tiring scramble up steep and loose terrain to gain

2hr 30min – Baisse du Basto (2693m), a broadish opening on an elevated elongated south–north ridge. At your feet is an awesome wild valley dominated by a jagged crest featuring Tête du Lac Authier due W.

Brace yourself for the knee-destroying descent, initially L. You pick your way across a succession of bare rock, scree and boulder-choked gullies, with the odd buttress scramble. ▸ Red/white markers are plentiful and clear, but watch your step, as this is precipitous terrain. Further down, at the confluence of forked valleys at the foot of Cime de la Fous is the first of a string of pretty lakes (2379m), a welcome change after all that stark rock.

Along a broad corridor a level path due W hugs the shores of two unnamed tarns, before reaching exquisite **Lac Niré** (2353m) under the impressive sharp point of Cime Niré.

Bearing NW, guided by cairns, it's steady but relatively easy going downhill to a gushing waterfall, where afternoon walkers will probably get their feet wet. The path drops across a bridge (P418) straddling the opening of Vallon de la Fous, where ibex graze or laze on the

Some snow cover can be expected early in the season, so keep your eyes open for markings.

Snow cover is likely at the start of the season.

Unnamed tarn below Baisse du Basto

green pasture. Now only a modest rise separates you from brand-new

1hr 30min – Refuge de Nice (2232m). CAF, sleeps 80, cold shower, open 15 June to 26 September. (**Note** The refuge has no telephone.)

VARIANT STAGE 2
Refuge des Merveilles to Relais des Merveilles

Walking Time	3hr 20min
Difficulty	Grade 2
Distance	7.7km/4.7 miles
Ascent/Descent	381m/911m

A straightforward alternative to the main route via Baisse du Basto, this crossing leads into wild Vallon d'Empuonrame, home to astonishingly tame herds of chamois and ibex. The ensuing descent to the floor of Vallée de la Gordolasque is long and rather tiring, and best taken slowly to ease pressure on the knees. However, at the end, a relaxing garden at the gîte awaits weary walkers.

From **Refuge des Merveilles** (2130m), as for the main route, take the well-trodden path due W above the lake. At **P93** ignore the fork R for the Vallée des Merveilles and turn L (WNW). This quickly becomes a gentle, perfectly graded ascent past the sheer side slab of Cime du Lac. Well above the treeline, Lac de l'Huile comes into view beneath Cime du Diable in a chaos of broken rock. Grassy basins are traversed, home to romping marmot colonies and multi-coloured violets. It's easy going, looping up to

1hr 20min – Pas de l'Arpette (2511m) and a vast outlook. Sharp L is craggy Cime des Verrairiers, while N is Mont des Merveilles. 'Arpette' is a variant of alpe, meaning 'pasture'.

This variant means missing upper Vallée de la Gordolasque and the surrounds of Refuge de Nice, but this is easily remedied by taking time out from the traverse and following the single-day route to the hut and lakes – see Walk 4.

67

Down the other side, the landscape is a completely different story – a rugged chaos of broken rock and wild crests. However a clear, decent path winds down, aided by timber reinforcements. Not far down, in Vallon d'Empuonrame, there is a sequence of basins, their sides smothered in pink alpenrose shrubs. ◀ In surprising contrast to this pastoral idyll is the gigantic green conduit that cuts across the valley ahead, bearing precious water all the way from Lac de la Fous at the foot of Monte Gelàs.

Once the path has crossed the stream it ducks under the pipeline. The valley at your feet is awesome, with sheer mountainsides plunging to a narrow floor. The U-shaping of glacial origin, modified to a V-profile by running water, is clear to see. Tight and narrow zigzags lead down an increasingly steep slope towards the floor

Families of chamois graze here, apparently heedless of the presence of humans.

At Pas de l'Arpette

68

Relais des Merveilles

of Vallée de la Gordolasque. Veering R (NW) over rubble, it finally enters shady wood, ending its crazy descent at

1hr 45min – Pont du Countet (1690m) (P411). Here there are glimpses N towards Mont Clapier and its neighbours, the 3000m-plus peaks on the Italo–French border. (Walk 4 to Refuge de Nice starts here.)

Turn L past the car park down the road, short-cutting a corner to

15min – Relais des Merveilles (1600m), a gîte d'étape where you can enjoy a drink in the garden. Comfortable rooms with en suites are on offer as well as dorms. ☎ (33) 049 3034355 open Easter to mid-October www. relaisdesmerveilles.com.

Pastoral Vallée de la Gordolasque continues to Roquebillière (gîte staff will call a taxi if needed) and buses in Vallée de Vésubie.

To continue on to Refuge Madone de Fenestre, see Variant Stage 3 below.

STAGE 3

Refuge de Nice to Madone de Fenestre

Walking Time	3hr 45min
Difficulty	Grade 3
Distance	5km/3.1 miles
Ascent/Descent	375m/704m

Another hard but spectacular day's walking – this time including 'impossibly' steep Pas Mont Colomb, which links upper Vallée de la Gordolasque with Vallon de la Madone de Fenestre. Giant of the Maritimes Monte Gelàs can be admired during the long descent, which finishes at a historic sanctuary with an excellent refuge. Be aware that late-lying snow is common on the W side of the pass, and icy in cold conditions.

Leave **Refuge de Nice** (2232m) along the red/white waymarked GR52, on the stepped way down the northern end of **Lac de la Fous**. Skirt the lake, then a rough track drops S past the dam wall, a favourite hang-out of ibex apparently in search of salt.

After an abandoned shepherds' hut and pasture, turn R at **P416** (2173m), the start of the relentless climb NW towards the pass, in the shadow of Mont Ponset. Initially grassy, the terrain gradually develops into a scree-field dotted with huge fallen boulders, the going inevitably slower and more tiring. The final 100m slog is over loose rocks, a demanding clamber verging on vertical in spots. A chimney finally terminates at

2hr – Pas Mont Colomb (2548m), a notch rather than a pass, hardly wide enough to stand up in! Perch on a rock to get your breath back and admire the vast outlook, including a glimpse of Argentera, NE, before facing the long – albeit slightly less steep – descent at your feet.

*At Pas Mont Colomb –
a gentler descent*

Tight zigzags plunge down the slope, and for early summer walkers there is a good chance of extensive snow patches. Keep a watchful eye out for waymarks as you traverse L to a huddle of rocks before dropping to a lake at 2390m, known to dry up in the course of a summer. Chamois herds abound in this wild valley, but keep their distance. Above NE rises Mont Colomb, while Ponset dominates SSE. A flatter, more relaxing stretch leads amidst grass and flowers.

A broad gully leads to a stream, and as you bear SW there are soon grandiose views of twin-peaked Monte Gelàs in all its glory. A short clamber and a traverse of chaotic rubble test ankles, at the foot of Caire de la Madone, streaked with lime-coloured lichen. Not far off is easier terrain, with larch and black vanilla orchids, on the last leg to a great waterfall and P367 junction. A few bridges later, fork R at Vacherie de la Madone for

1hr 45min – Madone de Fenestre (1903m). Next to the historic church and sanctuary (see 'Valleys and Bases in France' under 'Exploring the Maritime Alps' in the Introduction, page 23) stands the refuge, its stark exterior

The pretty valley near Madone de Fenestre

belying a warm, hospitable establishment that serves delicious food such as melt-in-the-mouth beef stew (☎ (33) 049 3028319 CAF, sleeps 62, open 18 June to 30 September, hot showers).

A midsummer shuttle bus links the sanctuary with St-Martin-Vésubie, 12km along the D94. Otherwise allow 3hr for the signed path to the village.

VARIANT STAGE 3
Relais des Merveilles to Madone de Fenestre

Walking Time	4hr
Difficulty	Grade 2
Distance	9.8km/6 miles
Ascent/Descent	845m/507m

Few other walkers are likely to be encountered on this rewarding alternative route. Trouble-free on clear paths, it is breathtakingly panoramic, with views to many 3000m-plus summits. The undisputed highlight is a meander around the delightful Lacs de Prals, in an off-shoot of Vallon de la Madone de Fenestre. The day's destination is a historic sanctuary and adjoining refuge where walkers are welcomed warmly and fed royally.

From **Relais des Merveilles** (1600m) turn downhill along the road past St-Grat chapel and a group of curious herders' huts, perfectly triangular in shape. At **P275** (10min) a lane breaks off R to lead uphill with occasional yellow markings. After power lines it becomes a clear path amidst conifers, spreads of juniper and lilac-flowering nettles.

Climbing NNW it leaves the shade of trees to traverse pasture slopes alternating with banks of pretty alpenrose interspersed with lichen-tinted rocks. After a shepherds'

Inspiring views from the Baisse de Prals ridge

hut the path ascends a broad crest colonised by juniper and iridescent alpine speedwell. Birds of prey are easily spotted on the open terrain, while alpine choughs chuckle overhead. A marvellous view of parallel blue-tinted ridges can be seen S, as the Maritime Alps begin their gentle descent towards the Mediterranean. Views up on the ridge are breathtaking – to Monte Gelàs and its entourage of spectacular jagged peaks.

Surrounded by zooming swallows only metres away L is

2hr – P365 (2335m), a short distance from Baisse de Prals. At your feet lies the attractive pasture basin Plan de Prals, enjoyed by cows and chamois alike.

Turn R (N) downhill on the zigzagging route for around 5min to where a clear if unmarked path forks R, cutting NNE across rock and earth. Endemic violets and bilberries abound. Over a modest crest is the marvellous basin housing

30min – Lacs de Prals (2269m), five photogenic lakes at the foot of the jagged profile and needle points of Mont Neiglier, its base a jumble of old moraine. Popular with picnickers and a thriving frog population.

It's a short climb to **Baisse des Cinq Lacs** (2335m) adjacent to Mont Caval. Awesome views take in Monte Gelàs and Col de Fenestre – you are surrounded by dizzy snow-spattered crests every way you look.

Lovely Vallon du Ponset awaits, the stepped way descending easily into larch and alpenrose, with views of the eponymous mount NE, and a dramatic waterfall. After a marshy basin the path plunges alongside an awesome gully eroded by water. You soon join contented cows grazing amidst giant tree roots and a pretty stream at P367. Turn L to cross several bridges to Vacherie de la Madone and P359. Fork R here for a short climb across rock slabs to

1hr 30min – Madone de Fenestre (1903m). See Stage 3 for information.

STAGE 4
Madone de Fenestre to Le Boréon

Walking Time	4hr 45min
Difficulty	Grade 2
Distance	11km/6.8miles
Ascent/Descent	545m/975m

A spectacular day, climbing first on an ancient mule track to a smugglers' pass, Pas des Ladres, and a vast Alpine outlook. An especially pretty lake is visited during the drop towards the valley floor and ancient forest, and a detour to beautifully placed Refuge de la Cougourde is possible. After a lengthy descent the stage concludes at the cluster of buildings that goes under the name Le Boréon, with both good gîte and hotel lodgings.

View from Pas des Ladres

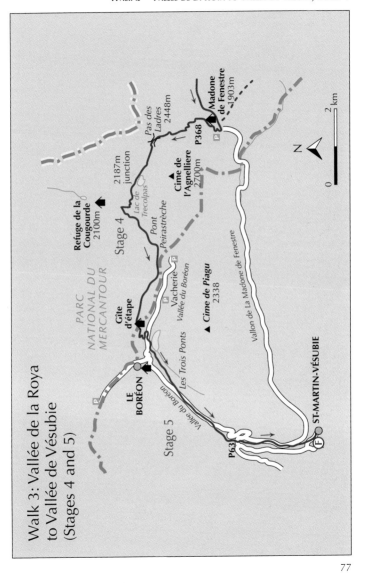

Walk 3: Vallée de la Roya
to Vallée de Vésubie
(Stages 4 and 5)

The Peirastreche waterfall

Leave **Madone de Fenestre** (1903m) on the beautifully maintained paved track. It leads NNE uphill in easy wide curves. ▶ The surroundings are simply magnificent, and the eye is inevitably drawn E to the crown of peaks encompassing Monte Gelàs and Maledie.

At signed junction **P368** (30min) keep straight on, ignoring the branch R for Col di Fenestre. The way zig-zags NNW, cutting a steep slope, traversing gradually to gain an upper amphitheatre. Across rubble-ridden terrain it gains

1hr 30min – Pas des Ladres (2448m). 'Pass of the thieves' was so named for the traders who came this way to avoid paying the taxes levied on their goods on major passes such as nearby Col de Fenestre. The vast outlook here takes in Monte Gelàs, Maledie and their neighbours ENE, as well as Mont Ponset and Neiglier SE. Close at hand is the walkers' peak Cime de l'Agnelliere (see Walk 6).

The descending path crosses loose rubble and earth, but quickly improves as it enters a lovely valley run through with trickling streams and dotted with pink flowering alpenrose shrubs. Gem-like **Lac de Trecolpas** (2150m) awaits, complete with its own mini island of conifers. ▶

The path continues NW over a glacially formed terrace, dropping below lake level to

45min – 2187m junction (P427) and an optional detour via Refuge de la Cougourde (see Walk 7).

Fork L (W) for the straightforward descent towards lush conifer wood, where you join the hut's access path well below the building. Turn L SSW alongside a cascading stream.

40min – Pont Peirastrèche. Ignore directions for the Vacherie and stick to the GR52 arrows without crossing the river.

Chamois and marmots are easily spotted in the treeless terrain, which also supports pink triffid-like houseleeks and alpine mouse-ear.

A picnic is definitely on the cards, and a dip may be considered, water temperature permitting.

The path narrows a bit and soon gives superb views of the Peirastrèche waterfall. Further down a lane is joined briefly, past private Refuge Saladin. At P380 the path ascends a little for a seemingly never-ending traverse WNW in woodland. At a minor waterfall you zigzag sharp L downhill, and soon the first chalets and signs of settlement are encountered. The path leads directly to the start of a minor road and

1hr 40min – Gîte d'étape Le Boréon, a lovely home-style establishment. ☎ (33) 049 3032727, sleeps 40, open May to September, on reservation for the rest of the year, hot shower, http://giteduboreon.monsite.wanadoo.fr.

Walk down the road to

10min – Le Boréon (1473m) with hotel accommodation on the lakeside. Grand Hotel Boréon ☎ (33) 049 3032035 www.hotel-boreon.com; Le Cavalet ☎ (33) 049 3032146.

STAGE 5
Le Boréon to St-Martin-Vésubie

Walking Time	1hr 30min
Difficulty	Grade 1–2
Distance	6.4km/3.9 miles
Descent	533m

This final stage involves a straightforward path, the Sentier Valléen de Vésubie, leading along the lake then down through thick forest. After a short stretch along the road – the detour caused by landslip and an unpassable path – it deposits you in the heart of the charming mountain town St-Martin-Vésubie.

Old square at St-Martin-Vésubie

The route continues on the other side of the road, but at the time of writing it was closed due to a landslip, so be prepared for about 1km of tarmac.

Leave **Le Boréon** (1473m) from the eastern end of the artificial lake (*barrage*). Take the path along the water's edge, but about halfway along climb up L to join the track with yellow markers. Amidst beautiful conifers you pass high above the dam itself, for the descent L (SW) in deep, cool forest. The stream and the D89 road are reached at **Les Trois Ponts** (30min, 1262m). ◄

Turn L downhill, and after several chalets, R next to a fence on an unmarked path that goes diagonally down to pick up the Sentier Valléen in cool, mixed woodland, following old stone walls. At P63 it crosses the main road and continues as a quiet, surfaced side-road through the start of the spread-out residential area of St-Martin. The D94 from Madone de Fenestre slots in and you quickly reach **St-Martin-Vésubie** (940m).

The 'Courmayeur of the Maritimes' has a fascinating old town centre, medieval in character. Also, a helpful tourist office, ATM, range of accommodation, restaurants, al fresco cafés, and supermarket and daily coach runs to Nice. Très agréable!

Hotel La Châtaigneraie ☎ (33) 049 3032122 www.raiberti.com
Gîte La Rouguiere ☎ (33) 049 3032919, sleeps 16 rouguiere@aol.com

WALK 4

Upper Vallée de la Gordolasque

Walking Time	5hr or 1 day
Difficulty	Grade 1–2
Distance	13.2km/8.2 miles
Ascent/Descent	689m/689m
Start/Finish	Pont du Countet
Access	Branching off Vallée de Vésubie and the D2565 near Roquebillière (nearest bus service), Vallée de la Gordolasque runs NW for 11km; the road terminates at Pont du Countet with a car park.

This wonderful day walk explores upper Vallée de la Gordolasque, where walkers are dwarfed by soaring pale-grey mountain ridges. Close to France's border with Italy, it features a cluster of peaks topping the 3000m mark, Mont Clapier in the lead. Glacial movement modelled the valley, rendering it severe in places, but the present deep V-profile is due to the captivating stream that cascades down stepped

Pont du Countet where the walk starts

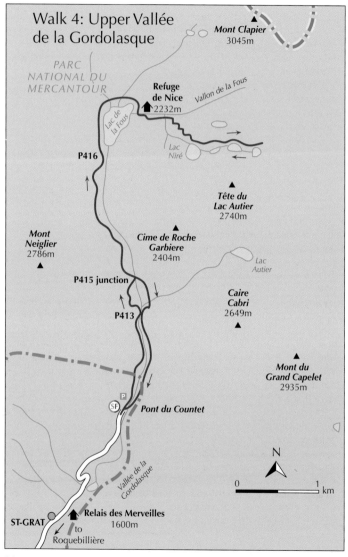

Walk 4: Upper Vallée de la Gordolasque

Mont Clapier
3045m

PARC NATIONAL DU MERCANTOUR

Refuge de Nice
2232m

Vallon de la Fous

Lac de la Fous

P416

Lac Niré

Tête du Lac Autier
2740m

Mont Neiglier
2786m

Cime de Roche Garbiere
2404m

Lac Autier

P415 junction

Caire Cabri
2649m

P413

Mont du Grand Capelet
2935m

Pont du Countet

N

ST-GRAT

Relais des Merveilles
1600m

to Roquebillière

Vallée de la Gordolasque

0 _____ 1
km

terraces. High up, pretty tarns nestle in high-altitude cirques, where snow and ice often persist into summer months. These are the day's destination, part of a grandiose Alpine landscape. First-class entertainment comes courtesy of remarkable numbers of ibex, chamois and marmots.

Good paths are followed throughout, with a sole short exception – half an hour into the walk, the route loops to the L of the waterfall for a short rock-slab traverse, but this is easily avoided – see below.

One of the Mercantour's most important huts, Refuge de Nice, is touched upon. Extended and re-opened in 2009 after a long period of renovation, it succeeds the 1889 Bivouac de la Barma and a 1902 shelter 'extravagantly' furnished with 10 wooden bunk beds, hay and blankets, and inaugurated by distinguished CAF Nice President De Cessole.

At the spread-out hamlet of St-Grat, 2km downhill from the walk start, is Relais des Merveilles, a perfect base for this walk.

WALK

Pont du Countet (1690m) marks your entrance into the Parc du Mercantour. Inspired by the great array of imposing peaks standing out on the skyline ahead, take the broad path on the L side of the stream (due N). It leads through the last of the trees, mostly Arolla pines that have taken root on fallen rocks, though the odd larch dots the stark mountainside in this steep-sided section. At a fork **P413** (30min) stick to the L side of the river. ▸

The clear path takes a wide curve over loose stone. Yellow alpine cabbage flourishes here, as do purple orchids and insectivorous butterwort, nourished by trickling water. A short, stepped stretch crosses a wet rock face with a little exposure. It's not far to the **P415 junction**. Up R are the tops of Pointes de l'Estrech, while ahead N is aptly named Mont Rond. Vast smoothed flanks and *roches mountonnées* streaked with lichen, contrast with gardens of pink alpenrose.

Follow cairns L briefly away from the main watercourse in a deep gully, to climb into a flat pasture where

Here you could opt for the easier path indicated by arrows for Refuge de Nice, pointing R across a bridge and to the R of the fall; the two routes join at P415 – timing is the same.

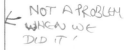

← NOT A PROBLEM WHEN WE DID IT !

In Vallon de la Fous

ibex graze and marmots romp. Raised timber walkways cross marshy areas. Ignore the turnoff (**P416**) for Pas Mont Colomb and cross abandoned pasture with a rudimentary shepherds' shelter. Approaching a dam wall, the path veers L up to **Lac de la Fous** (2173m), which is circled. Clumps of bulbous gentians brighten the shore.

Paved steps lead up to brand-new **Refuge de Nice** (2232m, 1hr 45min). A wonderful perch affording great views towards a series of giants, dominated by Mont Clapier, NE – but there's better to come!

Proceed uphill (E) on the well-trodden path, over a rise into a beautiful grassy basin, Vallon de la Fous. After a bridge (P418) it's SE and uphill over rocks to a great waterfall where you can expect to get your boots wet. Cairns point up to the magnificent setting of **Lac Niré** (2353m, 30min). ▶

With a little clambering over fallen rocks, the way continues on a level due E to three further lakes, the last (2379m) in Vallon du Mont Chaminaye, at the foot of the eponymous peak – just one in the marvellous crown enclosing this amphitheatre. Snow can lie late here, adding to the fascination.

Return the same way to **Refuge de Nice** then the **P415 junction** (1hr 30min). Here you need to fork L and ford the stream. Soon over a rise is the curious 'Mur des italiens', an old military wall barrier. Then you zigzag down for a spectacular view of the waterfall.

Further on the path negotiates a cascading stream before reaching the **P413 fork**. Keep on this side of the river, now on what used to be a road. A little way on, take care to follow cairns R for the path leading through to the wooden bridge **Pont du Countet** (1690m, 45min) and not far on, the car park.

While apparently from *noir* ('black'), a reference to the dark colouring of the surrounding rocks, reliable studies link the name to the dialect word for marmot. Soaring above are Tête du Lac Autier and Cime Niré.

Relais des Merveilles ☎ (33) 049 3034355, open Easter to mid-October www.relaisdesmerveilles.com.
Refuge de Nice, CAF, sleeps 80, cold shower, open 15 June to 26 September. (**Note** The refuge has no telephone.)

WALK 5
Lacs de Prals Circuit

Walking Time	3hr 30min or 1 day
Difficulty	Grade 1–2
Distance	6.2km/3.8 miles
Ascent/Descent	700m/700m
Start/Finish	P361 on the roadside 1km below Madone de Fenestre
Access	From St-Martin-Vésubie it's 12km on the D94 to the sanctuary of Madone de Fenestre; a shuttle bus covers the route in midsummer. Roadside parking.

A wonderful circuit that leads up to the five pretty Lacs de Prals and glorious views of 3000m-plus stone giants of the Maritime Alps. This is easily fitted into a leisurely day, and should ideally include a picnic in the lovely basin where the lakes lie. A longer variant loop is possible, via the broad crests and peaks ringing Plan de Prals – allow 5hr 30min total (see below). 'Prals' derives from 'meadow'.

At the walk's end is a refuge and the historic church-cum-sanctuary of Madone de Fenestre – (see 'Valleys and Bases in France' under 'Exploring the Maritime Alps' in the Introduction, page 23). Walk 6 also begins here.

WALK
En route to Madone de Fenestre, shortly before the last bend is **P361** (1807m). Here a signed path breaks off SW past a Mercantour Park signboard. Immersed in sweet-smelling pine forest, the going is leisurely, and mostly level as you round the vast base of Mont Caval. After a side-path (from Vacherie du Devense) slots in, the gradient steepens marginally as you enter Vallon de Prals SE. In a landscape with plentiful signs of ancient glacier moulding, terracing and cirques, the attractive pasture basin Plan de Prals is reached. Well-watered, it is enjoyed by cows and chamois alike.

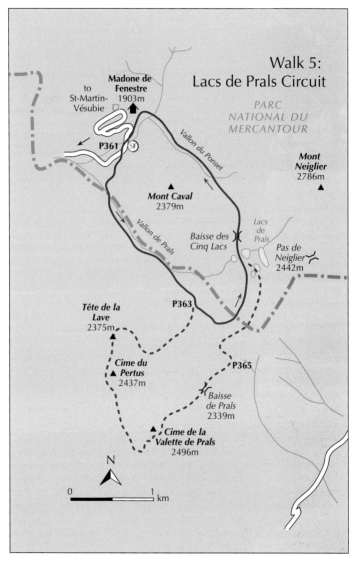

Walk 5:
Lacs de Prals Circuit

*PARC
NATIONAL DU
MERCANTOUR*

Madone de
Fenestre
1903m

to
St-Martin-
Vésubie

P361

SF

Vallon du Ponset

*Mont
Neiglier*
2786m

▲
Mont Caval
2379m

Vallon de Prals

*Baisse des
Cinq Lacs*

*Lacs
de
Prals*

*Pas de
Neiglier*
2442m

P363

*Tête de la
Lave*
2375m
▲

P365

▲ *Cime du
Pertus*
2437m

*Baisse
de Prals*
2339m

▲ *Cime de la
Valette de Prals*
2496m

N

0   1
└─────────┘ km

P363 (2063m, 1hr) marks the start of the variant loop.

Variant Loop via Cime de la Valette de Prals to Lacs de Prals (2hr 30min)
A clear but steep path strikes out SW, making its way up to **Tête de la Lave** (2375m), a marvellous vantage point with wide-reaching views. You go SSE, skirting Cime du Pertus, then ascend to the triangle of **Cime de la Valette de Prals** (2496m), overlooking Vallée de la Gordolasque. Along the ~~razor~~ crest NE, make your way down to **Baisse de Prals** (2339m) and nearby junction **P365**. Turn L (N) downhill on the zigzagging route for 5min, to where a clear if unmarked path forks R, cutting NNE across rock and earth, brightened by endemic violets and bilberry shrubs. Over a modest crest is the marvellous basin housing the **Lacs de Prals** (2269m).

Here, extraordinary views take in Monte Gelàs and the historic Col de Fenestre pass, with dizzy snow-spattered crests every way you look.

A little further up, at **P364** (2149m), fork L for the gradual climb to the basin holding the **Lacs de Prals** (2269m, 30min), and spreads of alpenrose. The dramatic backdrop consists of towering Mont Neiglier and a procession of needle-like peaks. This is a perfect spot for a picnic, though the lakes are a little too shallow for swimmers – frogs apart. A short climb N takes you to **Baisse des Cinq Lacs** (2335m), a broad saddle alongside Mont Caval. ◄

Scenic descent in Vallon du Ponset

Lacs de Prals backed by Mont Neiglier

Below is lovely Vallon du Ponset, with a stepped path easing the descent. Larch and alpenrose soon appear, as does the eponymous mount NE and a dramatic waterfall. A flat marshy basin is crossed on stepping-stones, before the path plunges alongside a gully and cascading stream. You soon join contented cows grazing amidst giant tree stumps, then a pretty stream at P367. Turn L to Vacherie de la Madone and P359. ▸

Fork R here for a short climb across rock slabs dotted with knobbly flowering houseleeks, to the historic sanctuary-church and old-style **Refuge Madone de Fenestre (1905m, 1hr 30min).** A good spot for a drink and snack or overnight stay.

From the car park take the short-cuts S to return to the start point **P361** (1807m, 15min).

Instead of crossing the bridge for the sanctuary, you could follow the wide track through to the road, then turn L for the few metres to P361 where you started – saving 30min.

Refuge Madone de Fenestre ☎ (33) 049 3028319 CAF, sleeps 62, open 18 June to 30 September, hot showers

WALK 6

Ancient Passes above Madone de Fenestre

Walking Time	3hr 30min or 1 day
Difficulty	Grade 2+
Distance	7.2km/4.5 miles
Ascent/Descent	570m/570m
Start/Finish	Madone de Fenestre
Access	From St-Martin-Vésubie it is 12km on the D94 to the sanctuary of Madone de Fenestre; a shuttle bus covers the route in midsummer.

Madone de Fenestre

Following this route means treading in the footsteps of many, many centuries of traders, pilgrims, soldiers, migrants and refugees. Col de Fenestre is a broad Alpine pass between Vallée de Vésubie (France) and Val Gesso (Italy), part of an ancient trade route connecting the Mediterranean coast with the vast Piemonte plain; salt

Walk 6: Ancient Passes above Madone de Fenestre

Col de Fenestre 2471m

Pas des Ladres 2448m

Lac de Fenestre

Cime de l'Agnelliere 2700m

PARC NATIONAL DU MERCANTOUR

P368

Madone de Fenestre 1903m

to St-Martin-Vésubie

N

0   1 km

was carried north to be traded against wool and skins. More recently – in 1943 – the pass witnessed the heartbreaking flight of 800 Jews into Italy. It was the immediate aftermath of the Italian Armistice, and they hoped for sanctuary, but many were rounded up by the SS and deported to camps, although people around Cuneo succeeded in sheltering and saving a fair number.

Starting at the beautifully located refuge and sanctuary of Madone de Fenestre (see 'Valleys and Bases in France' under 'Exploring the Maritime Alps' in the Introduction, page 23), this magnificent day route takes a historic mule track to climb effortlessly to Col de Fenestre and France's border with Italy. Next comes a superb traverse on an old military path to a smuggler's pass and an optional walker's peak. Panoramas are brilliant the whole time, including far-reaching views to a good line-up of 3000m-plus Maritime peaks; chances of sighting wildlife are excellent. Clear paths are followed mainly, with just the odd narrow stretch that can feel a little exposed, during the high traverse.

A note concerning the name: as well as the rock 'window' in the legend (see Introduction), another contender for the origin of 'Fenestre' is the Latin *'finisterrae'* or 'end of the world', which this place may well have felt like to the inhabitants in medieval times.

WALK

Chamois and marmots are easily spotted on the treeless terrain, which also supports pink triffid-like houseleeks and alpine mouse-ear.

Leave **Madone de Fenestre** (1903m) on the paved track, which is beautifully restored. Wide curves lead effortlessly uphill NNE. ◀ The surroundings are magnificent and the eye is inevitably drawn E to the crown of peaks encompassing Cime Gelas and Maledie.

At signed junction **P368** (30min) – where the return path slots in – fork R across the stream. Views E stretch to Mont Colomb and its col, as well as prominent Ponset ESE. At 2266m the path dips into an attractive basin holding inviting **Lac de Fenestre** – a brief level respite before the climb continues.

A little further up keep R at an unmarked fork, then you pass old concrete bunkers, relics of fascist paranoia, now popular shelters for ibex who are oblivious of man-made history. A little before the actual col is junction **P369**, then it's only minutes up to **Col de Fenestre** (2476m, 1hr) and the Franco–Italian border. Nestling on the northern flanks are more barracks, along with a magnificent outlook N along the jagged crests of the Parco delle Alpi Marittime, Cime du Lombard standing out close by, NNW.

Return to nearby junction **P369**, but now turn R for the traverse, a former military mule track cutting SW high across the head of the valley. Flights of stone steps wind up and down, the odd stretch a little dizzying, but extremely enjoyable.

Bunker en route to Col de Fenestre

Pas des Ladres (2448m, 30min) – 'pass of the thieves' – refers to the traders who used this secondary pass to avoid paying the taxes levied on their goods at the major passes. Now the panorama takes in Monte Gelàs, Maledie, and their neighbours ENE, as well as Ponset and Neiglier SE. At your feet nestles renowned Lac de Trecolpas, its shores dotted with picnickers. ▸

The descent route heads due S to traverse a rubble slope, before zigzagging down to the **P368** junction encountered earlier on. The wide track leads back to where you started at **Madone de Fenestre** (1903m, 1hr 30min).

Anyone with a sure foot and the time and inclination to see more can follow the optional extension to 2700m **Cime de l'Agnelliere**. The clear if narrow path quickly climbs SW – allow 1hr 30min return.

Refuge Madone de Fenestre ☎ (33) 049 3028319 CAF, sleeps 62, open 18 June to 30 September, hot showers

WALK 7
Vallon du Haut Boréon Circuit

Walking Time	4hr 10min or 1 day
Difficulty	Grade 2
Distance	9km/5.6 miles
Ascent/Descent	521m/521m
Start/Finish	Vacherie du Boréon car park
Access	From St-Martin-Vésubie it is 11km on the D2565 then the D89 past lakeside Le Boréon to the Vacherie du Boréon.

A fantastic circular walk on good paths through beautiful forest following a cascading river that is straight out of a picture book. Above the treeline is a near-perfect tarn, Lac de Trecolpas, a haven for picnickers. The ensuing traverse leads to a lovely refuge in a high-altitude cirque crowned by impressive peaks. (Here Walk 8 climbs on an arduous path to the marvellous, solitary Lacs Bessons.) You return to the valley for the walk conclusion at the Vacherie car park – all in all, a great day out.

The scatter of buildings that makes up Le Boréon includes a friendly gîte d'étape and two restaurant/hotels on the edge of the modest dam-cum-lake.

WALK

From the lower car park at **Vacherie du Boréon** (1629m) take the path via the upper parking area and P420, then the broad way climbing gradually E into Vallon du Haut Boréon. At P421 ignore the Mairis turn-off; you soon enter the realms of the Parc du Mercantour. The route coasts NE through forest, following the R bank of a beautiful river that crashes over a waterfall further upstream in the vicinity of Chalet Vidron. Then, on **Pont de Peirastrèche** (1838m, 50min), you cross to the opposite bank. (The curious name in Provencal means 'a place with narrow rocky cliffs'.) Here you join forces with the GR52, and continue close to the gently cascading waterway lined by conifers.

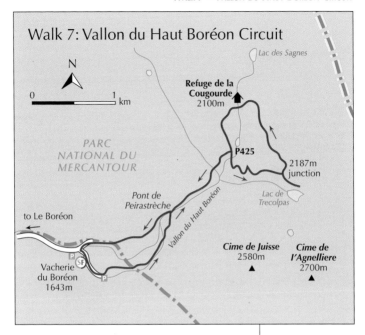

Walk 7: Vallon du Haut Boréon Circuit

Lac des Sagnes

N

0   1 km

Refuge de la Cougourde
2100m

P425

PARC
NATIONAL DU
MERCANTOUR

2187m
junction

*Pont de
Peirastrèche*

Lac de
Trecolpas

to Le Boréon

Vallon du Haut Boréon

Cime de Juisse
2580m
▲

*Cime de
l'Agnelliere*
2700m
▲

Vacherie
du Boréon
1643m

Not far up, shortly after P424 for the Lacs Bessons route, you reach an old grazing spot, Gias de Peirastrèche, and **P425** (1936m) – fork R here to re-cross the river. This becomes a steady climb, essentially E, to the edge of the treeline and a **2187m junction** (P427, 2187m). Turn R here for a short stretch over rocky terrain, an ancient glacial terrace, into the upper cirque that hosts pretty **Lac de Trecolpas** (2150m, 1hr 30min). This is a gem of a lake set in a huge amphitheatre overseen by vast ridges and tumbled boulders – perfect for a family picnic and even a dip, water temperature permitting.

Backtrack to the 2187m junction (P427), but keep straight on (N), remaining high – initially across stone blocks, then on a very pretty path cutting steep mountainside dotted with larch trees, and an unbeatable spread of delicate pink alpenrose shrubs. A cascading

Refuge de la Cougourde

stream is crossed as you gain **Refuge de la Cougourde** (2100m, 40min), standing on the southernmost lip of one of the most appealing cirques in the whole of the Maritime Alps. It is crowned by elegant Caires de Cougourde, known simply as 'the Cougourde' to the tribe of climbers who are drawn to its sheer faces. The name derives from a Celtic term for a type of gourd or pumpkin, probably in view of the mountain's shape. As for the hut, the attractive timber building was inaugurated in 2003, a cosy place that meets high environmental standards. Chamois and ibex mingle freely on rock slabs nearby, drawn in by the salt supplied by the hut staff.

The return route drops quickly in curves S down Vallon du Haut Boréon, to Gias de Peirastrèche (1936m), where you forked off earlier on. This time, go downhill to **Pont de Peirastrèche** (1838m), but instead of crossing the bridge, stick to the R bank of the river for the narrow path in common with the GR52. ◄

Not far along there are superb views of the waterfalls.

A steepish stretch through thick wood, with a twist of tree roots underfoot, ends at a lane. Turn sharp L here (if you reach private hut Refuge Saladin and P380 you've gone too far) across the river and return to the car park at **Vacherie du Boréon** (1629m, 1hr 15min).

Gîte du Boréon ☎ (33) 049 3032727, sleeps 40, open May to September, on reservation for the rest of the year, hot shower http://giteduboreon.monsite.wanadoo.fr
Refuge de la Cougourde CAF, sleeps 42, open 15 June to 30 September, hot showers (**Note** The refuge has no telephone.)

Le Boréon
Grand Hotel Boréon ☎ (33) 049 3032035 www.hotel-boreon.com
Le Cavalet ☎ (33) 049 3032146

WALK 8
Lacs Bessons

Walking Time	5hr 30min or 1 day
Difficulty	Grade 3
Distance	10km/6.2 miles
Ascent/Descent	952m/952m
Start/Finish	Vacherie du Boréon car park
Access	From St-Martin-Vésubie, 11km on the D2565 then the D89 past lakeside Le Boréon and then to the Vacherie du Boréon.

This breathtaking route climbs to the 2500m mark amidst the magnificent procession of lofty Maritime peaks lined up along the Franco-Italian border. These dizzy north-ernmost reaches of Vallon du Haut Boréon are little fre-quented and wonderfully wild. Your destination is the superb and much-photographed Lacs Bessons – the name means 'twin' in Provencal dialect – nestling in a deep basin that is snow- and ice-bound well into summer. En route, there are magnificent conifer forests, cascading torrents and a string of pretty Alpine lakes to enjoy.

The going is a steep slog in parts, with numerous stream crossings entailing wobbly stepping-stones and a bit of leaping, so trekking poles come in handy. What's more it's a long climb – almost 1000m – for a single day outing, so do consider overnighting at Refuge de la Cougourde and stretching it out over two days. Good weather with clear visibility is essential, due to the lack of landmarks high up, where it's easy to lose your way.

For Le Boréon accommodation see Walk 7, an easier circuit in the Vallon du Haut Boréon.

WALK

From the upper car park at **Vacherie du Boréon** (1670m) take the broad path for a gentle ascent into Vallon du Haut Boréon entering the Parc du Mercantour. Heading NE through forest, you follow the R bank of a beautiful river that crashes over a waterfall further upstream. The path crosses L over **Pont de Peirastrèche** (1838m, 40min) to join forces with the GR52, continuing in the same direction close to the gently cascading river. Not far up, shortly after P424, where the return slots in later, you reach Gias de Peirastrèche. Ignore turn-offs and continue uphill to emerge at

Stream crossing below Lacs Bessons

Walk 8: Lacs Bessons

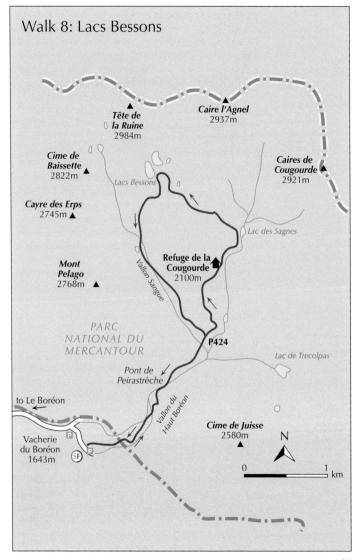

Tête de
la Ruine
2984m

Caire l'Agnel
2937m

Cime de
Baissette
2822m

Caires de
Cougourde
2921m

Cayre des Erps
2745m

Lacs Bessons

Lac des Sagnes

Mont
Pelago
2768m

Refuge de la
Cougourde
2100m

Vallon Sangue

PARC
NATIONAL DU
MERCANTOUR

P424

Lac de Trecolpas

Pont de
Peirastrèche

Vallon du
Haut Boréon

to Le Boréon

Cime de Juisse
2580m

N

Vacherie
du Boréon
1643m

0   1
km

Refuge de la Cougourde (2100m, 1hr 20min). Rebuilt in 2003 to strict environmental standards, the cosy hut is located on the edge of a lovely cirque run through with streams and surmounted by striking peaks, notably the smoothed outline of the Caires de Cougourde, or 'the Cougourde' for the climbers who flock to its sheer walls. The name apparently derives from a type of gourd.

Only metres before the hut, turn R (NW) to follow the bank of a stream all the way to a waterfall, keeping an eye out for faint markers and path. You climb easily to the L of the fall on grassy terrain, reaching pretty **Lac des Sagnes** (2198m) below the Cougourde and Caire l'Agnel. Without actually crossing the lakes, bear L (NNW), hunting out cairns leading to the base of a rock incline.

Now begins the straightforward if constantly steep route mostly NW. There's a lot of hands-on clambering, but no exposure. Up ahead N soars Tête des Lacs Bessons, the rocky top of which provides a good reference point, as you'll be passing well to its L. Broad rubble gullies alternate with terraces, home to colourful red vanilla orchids, alpine butterwort and tall dark blue-green grasses.

At 2516m Tête de la Ruine looms NW and you reach an unnamed tarn. Orientation can be a little confusing – proceed essentially NW, clambering over rocks, with the odd path marker here and there. As you gain a broad, smooth-topped ridge and the highest point – 2580m – the twin Bessons lakes will come into view at your feet in their respective basins. The smaller, higher tarn feeds the lower body of water with cascades. What a breathtaking spot – on top of the world!

Head downhill making for the L (S) end of the larger and lower of **Lacs Bessons** (2541m, 1hr 40min) – a glorious place for a well-earned picnic. The path marked on the IGN map begins here, close to the lake outlet. Initially in a rock corridor away from the stream, it descends Vallon des Lacs Bessons S in tight zigzags on loose terrain – watch your step.

Down at the 2300m mark, you cross R over the stream and the path improves a little. At the valley's confluence

Lacs Bessons and Tête de la Ruine

with Vallon de Baissette, below polished rock slabs you approach a grassy basin with streams running through it. NNW is the distinctive point of Cime Baissette. A stream crossing takes you to the R bank of Vallon Sangue. In view SE are paired Cime de Juisse and Cime de l'Agnel, and stark grey elongated ridges.

The way continues SE, in the company of running water and greenery. A traverse L leads to a modest rise, with brilliant views to the Cougourde and Trecolpas valleys. Next comes a drawn-out knee-bashing descent in the shade of larch trees, many of which are magnificent old specimens. This finally terminates at 1871m and **P424** (1hr 30min) as the main path is rejoined at last.

Now head SSW, retracing your earlier steps via **Pont de Peirastrèche**, and back to the car park at **Vacherie de Boréon** (1670m, 1hr).

Refuge de la Cougourde CAF, sleeps 42, open 15 June to 30 September, hot showers (**Note** The refuge has no telephone.)

Path in Vallon Sangue

WALK 9
Around the Argentera

Walking Time	21hr or 4 days
Difficulty	Grade 2+
Distance	46.7km/28.9 miles
Ascent/Descent	3384m/3384m
Start/Finish	Le Boréon
Access	From St-Martin-Vésubie, 8km on the D2565 then the D89 to Le Boréon.

This exhilarating trek takes walkers on a strenuous four-day route from France into Italy and back again, circling the majestic Argentera – 'monarch of the Maritimes' for mountaineer WM Conway in 1894. Extending north–south for almost 1km, it peaks at 3297m with Cima Sud. (An altitude easily summoned up, as it is 'three metres less than three thousand three hundred'.) This was first successfully scaled in 1879 by the indefatigable Rev WA Coolidge, with the expert Swiss guides Almer father and son (see also Stage 2). However, the honour was his by a mere cat's whisker, as only the previous year young English mountaineer DW Freshfield had scaled adjacent (and till then untouched) Cima di Nasta, mistaking it for the summit.

Massive height gains and losses are clocked up en route, but all effort is well rewarded by magnificent vistas. Most of the cols traversed are little visited, so walkers can look forward to having vast wild valleys and their fascinating animal and bird life to themselves. Mid to late summer is advisable for this route – unless you especially enjoy glissades on the snow.

It is just as feasible to begin on the Italian side of the Maritimes, for instance at Terme di Valdieri in Stage 2. This sleepy old-style spa resort, founded by the royal family in the 1850s, makes a perfect alternative entry point, and is served by buses throughout summer. Done this

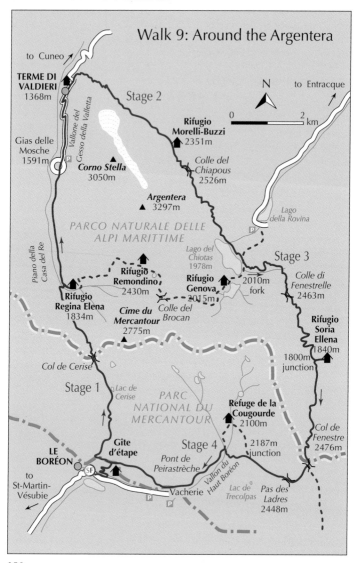

Walk 9: Around the Argentera

to Cuneo

TERME DI VALDIERI 1368m

Stage 2

to Entracque

N

0   2 km

Gias delle Mosche 1591m

Corno Stella 3050m

Vallone del Cesso della Valletta

Rifugio Morelli-Buzzi 2351m

Colle del Chiapous 2526m

Argentera 3297m

Lago della Rovina

PARCO NATURALE DELLE ALPI MARITTIME

Lago del Chiotas 1978m

Stage 3

Piano della Casa del Re

Rifugio Remondino 2430m

Rifugio Genova 2015m

2010m fork

Colle di Fenestrelle 2463m

Rifugio Regina Elena 1834m

Cime du Mercantour 2775m

Colle del Brocan

Rifugio Soria Ellena 1840m

1800m junction

Col de Cerise

Stage 1

Lac de Cerise

PARC NATIONAL DU MERCANTOUR

Refuge de la Cougourde 2100m

Col de Fenestre 2476m

LE BORÉON

Gîte d'étape

Stage 4

Pont de Peirastrèche

2187m junction

to St-Martin-Vésubie

Vacherie

Vallon du Haut Boréon

Lac de Trecolpas

Pas des Ladres 2448m

way, it allows you to soak in relaxing thermal water at the end of the trek! On the other hand, in lieu of Stage 2, which loses a lot of height descending to the valley floor, an excellent variant via Rifugio Remondino cuts over a southern shoulder of the Argentera on Colle del Brocan – see below. It rejoins the main route on Stage 3 at Rifugio Genova.

As well as the hotels (see Walk 8) at the start of the walk at Le Boréon, walkers will enjoy the company at the convivial gîte d'étape, a short way up the road (see below).

STAGE 1
Le Boréon to Rifugio Regina Elena

Walking Time	5hr 15min
Difficulty	Grade 2
Distance	8.8km/5.4 miles
Ascent/Descent	1070m/709m

A stiff but problem-free climb on clear paths via a dizzy pass out of France's Vésubie valley and into Italy in the company of magnificent lofty mountains. The stage ends at a basic but welcoming hut (where at least one day's advance warning is necessary if you'd like dinner). Otherwise hotel accommodation can be enjoyed 1hr 30min further down the valley at the Terme di Valdieri – see Stage 2.

Should you feel up to an additional 2hr climb, you can labour on from Rifugio Regina Elena to Rifugio Remondino via a variant route – see Walk 12, end of Stage 3.

From the lakeside at **Le Boréon** (1473m) follow the road past the Alpha wolf park and fork L uphill. It's not far for the branch R to

15min – Gîte d'étape Le Boréon, a home-style establishment, ☎ (33) 049 3032727, sleeps 40, open May to September,

on reservation for the rest of the year, hot shower http://
giteduboreon.monsite.wanadoo.fr.

The signed path begins next to the building. Initially NE,
it passes chalets and takes a short concrete ramp to the
park border and junction **P371** (1588m), where you turn
L. Amidst beautiful conifer forest with ancient gnarled
trees, you climb easily NW to enter Vallon du Cavalet.
Cow bells resound as you veer N on the approach to
Vacherie du Cavalet, which remains out of sight.

Keep straight on at P374, below the long ridge of
Serre des Gardes. The trees thin as the path enters a vast
rubble cirque headed by Cimes de Cerise, the pass a
clear notch visible ahead to their L. Under the watchful
eye of chamois, the path crosses masses of shattered rock
and touches on **Lac de Cerise** (2223m).

Ignore the turn-off for the popular destinations Lac
du Mercantour and the eponymous peak, which gave its
name to the French park. Over broken reddish rock the
way is marked by cairns. It swings briefly NW at the foot
of an old concrete bunker for the final slog to magnificent
views at

3hr 15min – Col de Cerise aka Colle Ciriegia (2543m),
which curiously means 'cherry', a reference to an old
name for Le Boréon, which has wild fruit trees around
it. In addition to marking the border between France
and Italy, naturally it is also the transition from the Parc
National du Mercantour to the Parco delle Alpi Marittime.
An old military building huddles, crumbling, on the north
side, not far from a plaque in memory of the refugees
who crossed in 1943. In the aftermath of the Second
World War, it also witnessed the passage of Italians strug-
gling to make ends meet by smuggling rice and leather
into France in exchange for precious salt.

The old mule track makes its way downhill in wide
curves through successive terraced cirques below the
Pagari peaks. Mostly NNW, it keeps to the L edge of the
valley. Huge slopes of shattered rocks and avalanche

En route to Col de Cerise (Stage 1)

Inspiring view from Col de Cerise

material are finally left behind and an earth path takes over, with alpenrose and spreads of yellow roseroot flowers. Vallone di Ciriegia stretches out at your feet, though your gaze will be drawn to the majestic, squarish Monte Matto NNW. Lower down the massive Argentera comes into sight.

Not far past a fork for the Fremamorta lakes, a rustic arrow points R for Rifugio Regina Elena, a final quarter of an hour. ◄

The faint path with white markings leads E across the rocky bed of a stream and through a thin spread of larch to

To continue directly to Piano della Casa del Re and then Terme di Valdieri, ignore this turn-off and continue N to join the rough road at 1735m where you pick up Stage 2.

1hr 45min – Rifugio Regina Elena (1834m). ☎ (39) 0171 97559 sleeps 14, open 15 June to 15 September, hot shower. A tiny, basic but welcoming hut named after a former Italian queen, and run by volunteer retired members of ANA, the Italian Association of Alpine Troops, who cook huge meals. It is beautifully placed for wonderful views up to the Argentera.

STAGE 2
Rifugio Regina Elena to Rifugio Morelli-Buzzi

Walking Time	4hr 45min
Difficulty	Grade 2
Distance	12.4km/7.7 miles
Ascent/Descent	983m/466m

A stroll down Vallone del Gesso della Valletta on a quiet road brings you out at the low-key mountain resort Terme di Valdieri, former haunt of royalty, hence the (once) Grand Hotel and hot springs. This relatively leisurely stretch is followed by – you guessed it – a stiff uphill to a homely hut below the northern shoulder of the Argentera massif.

Those intending to follow the variant to Rifugio Remondino and the Colle del Brocan traverse will need to turn off the main route almost immediately and continue with Walk 12, end of Stage 3.

Leave **Rifugio Regina Elena** (1834m) by way of the path that drops N across the streambed and up to a track. (This is where the access path for Rifugio Remondino turns R.) Keep L (NE) for the rough road across **Piano della Casa del Re** (20min, 1743m). At the base of the Argentera massif, it proceeds due N past playful marmots and laburnum trees, as well as the turn-off at **Gias delle Mosche** (1591m, for Rifugio Bozano – see Walk 15).

With the towering crests of San Giovanni flanking the western edge of the valley, the road, partially surfaced, descends imperceptibly at first, before a series of wide curves and the occasional short-cut. Through beautiful beech woods the minor road in Vallon del Gesso is reached.

1hr 30min – Terme di Valdieri (1368m). Turn L to reach the spa and accommodation: Hotel Royal ☎ (39) 0171 97106, www.termedivaldieri.it, open June to September,

111

hotel rooms and walkers' hostel (*posto tappa* GTA, sleeps 24, meals at hotel). A short distance further up the road is family-run Hotel Turismo ☎ (39) 0171 97334, open late April to September.

The bagni (spa baths) here make the most of 32 gushing springs, at 26–69°C, for the benefit of sufferers of ailments of the skin and respiratory system. Probably known to the Romans, it was not until the 16th century that a resort grew up. However, the present stately buildings are from 1857, the time of King Vittorio Emanuele II. Dominating the spa is Monte Matto, the name deriving from ancient Ligurian for 'heap of stones', rather than 'crazy' as suggested by modern Italian.

The walk continues by turning R at the rear of the hotel buildings, then R again through the car park. A signed path (in common with the GTA) branches off for Rifugio Morelli-Buzzi, soon crossing a footbridge at the base of Vallone di Lourousa. Through shady mixed woodland a steady climb SE follows on an old mule track with endless bends. Deserted Gias Lagarot (1917m) is passed, then a landmark boulder plastered with plaques to perished mountaineers.

Piano della Casa del Re

About halfway, the lovely grassy basin **Lagarot di Lourousa** (1970m), with its stream, affords a superb view up to notorious Canale di Lourousa. This vertiginous 45° gully, rising 900m in height and occupied by a tongue of ice, has claimed the life of many a climber on the Argentera massif. Incredibly, this was the route taken by Coolidge and the Almers on their pioneer ascent of the massif. On the other hand, Corno Stella, the 3050m rectangular-topped peak alongside Catene delle Guide at the culmination of the gully, was first scaled in 1903 by Count Victor De Cessole. ▶

Continue inexorably upwards, past the last weather-beaten trees and beneath increasingly imposing mountains, to the bare stony environs of

3hr 15min – Rifugio Morelli-Buzzi (2351m) ☎ (39) 0171 973940 CAI sleeps 45, open 15 June to 30 September, hot shower. This is a popular base for climbers attempting the Argentera, so remember to book ahead for weekend stays. The first hut on this site was erected in 1931, and has since been modernised.

The Terme di Valdieri

At their foot is tiny red Bivacco Varrone, a life-saving stopover for mountaineers.

STAGE 3
Rifugio Morelli-Buzzi to Rifugio Soria Ellena

Walking Time	5hr 30min
Difficulty	Grade 1
Distance	12.5km/7.7 miles
Ascent/Descent	658m/1169m

Two cols are traversed in this stage – and that of course means a double load of downs and ups! Former royal game tracks are the order of the day, as are magnificent expansive views of two of the Maritime record holders – the Argentera then Gelàs. At day's end is a hospitable refuge for the final overnight stay in Italy. This stage follows the same route as the long-distance GTA route.

Note The day's load is easily reduced by taking the short detour to Rifugio Genova for an overnight stay, as explained below. It's about halfway.

From **Rifugio Morelli-Buzzi** (2351m) a good path leads SSE, overshadowed by the sheer flanks of Monte Stella. Over rubble slopes it's fairly steep – and may be snow covered in early summer – to

40min – Colle del Chiapous (2526m), the name derived from 'slabs of rock'. Here horizons open up to reveal the craggy grey Fenestrelle ridges and twin-peaked Gelàs with its remnant snowfield SSE.

The clear path moves off S, at first coasting across a broad saddle (where it ignores a fork for Passo del Porco) before heading SE down the Vallone del Chiapous. Far below, soon can be seen the artificial lake Chiotas. The way is straightforward, on the remains of an old game track that descends a big gully in wide swinging curves. The surroundings of long-fallen rock are home to inquisitive chamois amidst hardy pink alpenrose, while many crannies shelter the delicate parsley fern. At the foot of Rocca Barbis you finally reach the

1hr 10min – dam wall (1980m). Not far along is a drop via a short tunnel under a concrete sluice channel, after which you need to turn R up the rough road.

> **Exit Route to Lago della Rovina (1hr 10min)**
> To leave the walk here, turn L (NE) down the rough road. Soon a junction offers two options: a knee-destroying drop due N or the more leisurely but longer track, occasionally subject to rock and earth slides (inadvisable during storms). Well below the Chiotas dam wall is Lago della Rovina (1535m) with a picnic area, snack bar and car park, where a midsummer shuttle bus operates to Entracque, a further 10km away by road.

Rifugio Genova's dramatic position

The road climbs back up to lake level for an easy stretch SE, which allows leisurely admiration of the soaring west faces of the Argentera. At a **fork (30 min, 2010m)**, branch L to leave the dirt road, unless you are ready to call it a day at nearby Rifugio Genova.

Detour to Rifugio Genova (15min)

Stick to the lakeside track that continues SW to Rifugio Genova (2015m) (☎ (39) 0171 978138, CAI, sleeps 60, open 15 June to 15 September, hot shower, credit cards www.rifugiogenova.it). The comfortable modern building was donated by the Electricity Commission to replace the 1898 hut, the very first of its kind in the Maritimes, submerged when the reservoir was constructed in the 1970s. It was named in honour of the Genoese branch of the Italian Alpine Club, who initiated the endeavour. It stands on glacially smoothed slabs on the shore of a natural lake at the foot of Vallone di Brocan.

Walkers on the variant via Colle del Brocan slot back in here.

Initially E amidst shrub vegetation and wildflowers, the path ascends Vallone di Fenestrelle surmounted by Roc di Fenestrelle SSE. Innumerable hairpin bends lead upward almost effortlessly in a vast semicircle beneath the imposing barrier of Rocce di Laura. A final stretch S leads across rainbow-coloured rock and past twin tarns preceding

1hr 30min – Colle di Fenestrelle (2463m). Surprisingly large numbers of ibex have made this superb col their summer abode.

The descent proceeds SSE in restful zigzags under Punta delle Lobbie, making its straightforward way downhill. Here the vast grassy slopes feed herds of chamois. Soon after the ruins of a herder's hut at Gias Alvé, finally, 600m beneath the col, you reach a huge boulder marking an **1800m junction** in Piano del Praiet. However, before you can enjoy that well-earned cool beer, a last (albeit short) uphill leg awaits to

1hr 40min – Rifugio Soria Ellena (1840m). ☎ (39) 0171
978382, CAI, sleeps 62, open 15 June to 15 September,
hot shower, www.rifugiosoriaellena.com. Welcoming
establishment, if a little cramped, where you'll be fed
royally.

Almost directly overhead is Gelàs, the 'Mont Blanc of
the Maritimes', whose 3142m peak was first scaled by
a group of aristocrats in far-off 1864. The name is a clear
reference to icy conditions, and also means 'curse' in
vernacular. In fact as the story goes, it was once the verdant home of three beautiful sisters who were subjected
to the unseemly attentions of men from Entracque. Their
end was tragically violent, and the mountain transformed
itself into an icy waste.

Gelàs has also lent its name to a liquor concocted
with bitter herbs, reputedly with digestive properties. Bird
lovers will be interested to know that these surroundings
offer excellent chances of spotting the awesome bearded
vulture, which is being re-introduced here.

*Rifugio Soria Ellena and
the descent path from
Colle di Fenestrelle*

STAGE 4
Rifugio Soria Ellena to Le Boréon

Walking Time	5hr 30min
Difficulty	Grade 2
Distance	13km/8.1 miles
Ascent/Descent	673m/1040m

The final stage of the trek sees you climb on a good path to the Italo–French border and a historic col, then embark on a stunning traverse to a smugglers' pass. A very long descent follows, via a pretty lake, through vast forest and pasture, finally reaching its conclusion at the hamlet of Le Boréon, where you started out four days ago. The walk can be drawn out a day longer – and this stage shortened marginally – by taking the detour to the stunningly located Refuge de la Cougourde (see below).

From **Rifugio Soria Ellena** (1840m) cut down to the valley floor and Piano del Praiet to pick up the rough stony track that heads due S up the broad valley. Moderately at first, it climbs at the foot of Cresta della Maura and in the shade of Cima del Lombard W in a stark, stony environment where grass becomes more and more scarce. Cliffs draw in as you proceed into Vallone di Finestra. ◄ A final gently sloping cirque is crossed to an old military barracks hugging the rock face only metres below

The jagged crest SE, linking Monte Gelàs with the pass ahead, can be seen.

2hr – Colle di Finestra or Col de Fenestre (2476m), which marks the border between Italy and France. The name 'finestra/fenestre' is linked to the revered sanctuary on the French side; the pass itself has been frequented

Exit to Madone de Fenestre (1hr 20min)
A clear wide track winds S down from the col to Madone de Fenestre (1903m), a sanctuary and refuge – see Walk 6.

since time immemorial by traders, pilgrims and refugees (see 'Valleys and Bases in France' under 'Exploring the Maritime Alps' in the Introduction, page 23).

On the French side of Col de Fenestre

A short way down into France, turn R at **P369** for an enjoyable traverse. The former military mule track cuts SW high across the head of the Vallon de Madone de Fenestre, with vast outlooks. Flights of stone steps wind up and down, the odd stretch a little dizzy, to gain

30min – Pas des Ladres (2448m, P428). 'Pass of the thieves' is a reference to the smugglers and traders who once used this secondary col to avoid paying the taxes levied on their goods at the main passes. The panorama takes in Monte Gelàs, Maledie and their neighbours ENE, as well as Neiglier SE.

Point your boots WNW down the loose rubble and earth path that leads into a beautiful valley, dotted with clumps of pink alpenrose and with streams running through. Down at 2150m is gem-like **Lac de Trecolpas**, complete with its own islands where conifers grow. ▶

This spot is very popular with picnickers – and even the odd daring bather.

119

The path leaves this lovely cirque and quickly comes to a

1hr – 2187m junction (P427) where it is feasible to detour to the memorable valley at the foot of the Cougourde mountain and cosy Refuge de la Cougourde – allow 30min, see Walk 7.

Turn L for the zigzags heading down into tree cover at last! After crossing a bridge, at P425 (1936m) it's L (SW) down Vallon du Haut Boréon following the cascading river. Stick to this bank, ignoring the Pont de Peirastrèche turn-off (1838m) for Vacherie du Boréon. In common with the GR52, the path narrows, and not far along gives superb waterfall views. After dropping steeply through thick wood with twisted tree roots underfoot, it emerges on a lane.

Keep R past a private hut (Refuge Saladin). A signed path soon continues WNW in a gentle ascent for a long traverse in light woodland. At a waterfall you zigzag down-hill at last, and follow signposting carefully through chalets and lanes, arriving at the Gîte d'étape Le Boréon (details in Stage 1). A short stroll down the road are hotels at

2hr – Le Boréon (1473m) where this rewarding trek began four days ago.

The Gîte du Boréon

WALK 10

Lac des Adus Loop

Walking Time	3hr 45min or 1 day
Difficulty	Grade 2+
Distance	8km/5 miles
Ascent/Descent	678m/678m
Start/Finish	Vallon de Salèse car park
Access	From St-Martin-Vésubie it's 8km on the D2565 then the D89 to Le Boréon and a further 3km up the narrow road in Vallon de Salèse.

This divine loop is indisputably one of the top walks in the Maritime Alps for the astonishingly vast panoramas it affords. Beautiful swathes of wood are traversed, giving way to jumbles of fallen rocks through which a path has been cleared, so that walkers can reach a high pass on the very edge of the Parc du Mercantour. Lac des Adus itself is a little further on – a deep green-blue gem of a lake embedded in conifer wood, close to the vast rockfall zone referred to as 'Les Adus'. The origin of the name is related to springs, in all probability *eau douce*, or 'fresh water'.

If on foot from the settlement of Le Boréon, allow an extra 1hr 50min (return time). Moreover, on the way up make sure you use the pretty path – in common with the GR52 – that leaves the road at P399.

Note On the last leg the zigzagging descent to the valley floor is steep, narrow and slippery in the wet. Take care.

WALK

From the traffic barrier and **car park** in Vallon de Salèse (1665m, P434), take the clear path marked 'Les Adus par Salèse'. Well trodden, it clings to the R side of the stream, WNW at first. ▶

During the gentle ascent a dirt road is touched on, then joined higher up beneath a steep eroded crest. Then it's a short stroll R to the big saddle **Col de Salèse** (1hr, 2031m).

The valley could be renamed 'valley of the bilberries' for the masses of juicy fruit it yields, embedded in showy spreads of pink alpenrose and shaded by larch.

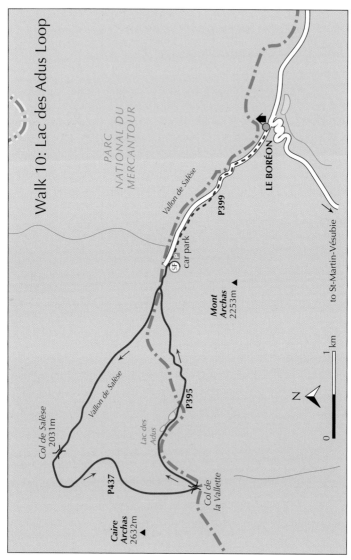

Walk 10: Lac des Adus Loop

PARC NATIONAL DU MERCANTOUR

Vallon de Salèse

P399

LE BORÉON

to St-Martin-Vésubie

car park

Mont Archas 2253m ▲

Vallon de Salèse

P395

Col de Salèse 2031m

Lac des Adus

P437

Caire Archas 2632m ▲

Col de la Vallette

N

0   1 km

Turn sharp L for a beautiful path SE via a grassy flower-strew shoulder dotted with pencil larch and pretty martagon lilies. As the trees start to thin there are gorgeous views to Monte Gelàs in the distant E, as well as the beautiful basins N holding the Fremamorta and Nègre lakes.

At P437 (turn-off for a short cut L/SE to Lac des Adus) continue upwards, venturing along the western edge of ancient rock falls. The way becomes rockier, but cairns are frequent, and soon it's a marvellous gentle traverse with continuing far-reaching vistas. ▶ Large green paint circles mark the border of the park, which you leave briefly to gain **Col de la Vallette** (1hr, 2356m). The Argentera, the highest peak in the Maritime Alps, is even visible from here – NE in the second row of peaks.

A clear descending path heads NNE, sticking closely to the park border. Masses of iridescent gentians and lilac crane's bill geraniums peek out of never-ending beds of flowers. At the foot of the chaotic rock falls nestles attractive if diminutive **Lac des Adus**

Rearing above halfway along is pointed Caire Archas. The open terrain is a good place for birdwatching, and eagles are not uncommon.

Mercantour border near Col de la Vallette

123

Lac des Adus is very popular with picnickers and the odd intrepid bather.

(30min, 2130m). ◄ Not far on is the P395 fork (where the short-cut joins up) and a cosy private chalet (Refuge des Adus). The path continues for a short stretch due E through Arolla pines.

Keep L at the P396 fork, to where the path narrows and all but plummets in innumerable hairpin bends down a rather steep flank. It occasionally feels a little exposed, and you need to watch your step at the odd landslip. With knees hopefully intact, you join the valley floor once again and fork R along the bank of the stream. Soon a bridge crosses L and you're back at the Vallon de Salèse **car park** (1hr 15min, 1665m). ◄

See Walk 7 for accommodation at Le Boréon.

Lac des Adus

WALK 11
The Great Lakes Tour

Walking Time	10hr 30min or 2 days
Difficulty	Grade 2–3
Distance	28.2km/17.5 miles
Ascent/Descent	1838m/1838m
Start/Finish	Vallon de Salèse car park
Access	From St-Martin-Vésubie, 8km on the D2565 then the D89 to Le Boréon. Here a narrow 3km leads up Vallon de Salèse.

A string of spectacular lakes in dramatic Alpine settings is encountered on this brilliant two-day circular route. Beginning with renowned Lac Nègre on the French side, it moves across to Italy to take in Lago delle Portette in a pretty steep-sided basin, and the photogenic Fremamorta tarns, which occupy shallow depressions left by ancient glacier pockets. Vast views are non-stop!

Note Be aware that the first trans-border crossing is by way of an especially precipitous pass (Pas de Préfouns), unsuitable for inexperienced walkers. Good weather is essential here, as the descent would be very difficult and dangerous in low visibility or adverse conditions.

The walk as described here starts from the Vallon de Salèse car park above Le Boréon, but it is just as feasible to begin from the Italian side, for instance from Vallon del Gesso della Valletta above the Terme di Valdieri – see Walk 14. It is also possible to link up with Walks 12 and 13.

If going on foot from the settlement of Le Boréon, allow an extra 1hr 50min in all. On the way up make sure you use the pretty path – which is also the GR52 – that leaves the road at P399. Accommodation possibilities at Le Boréon can be found under Walk 7.

Lago delle Portette

Walk 11: The Great Lakes Tour

PARCO NATURALE DELLE ALPI MARITTIME

Lac Valcuca

to Terme di Valdieri

Val Morta junction

2200m junction

Lago delle Portette

Rifugio Questa 2388m

Gias delle Mosche 1591m

Colletto del Valasco 2429m

Testa di Tablasses ▲

Lago inferiore di Fremamorta

Testa di Bresses ▲

Lago mediano di Fremamorta

Pas de Préfouns 2620m

Lago superiore di Fremamorta

○ **Bivacco Guiglia**

Stage 1

Pointe Giegn ▲ 2888m

Lac de Bresses

Lac Nègre

Stage 2

Caire Pounchu ▲ 2495m

Camp Soubran

Cima di Frémamorta ▲

◡ Colle di Fremamorta 2615m

Lacs de Frémamorte

Caire de Rogué ▲ 2705m

✕ *Col de Salèse*

PARC NATIONAL DU MERCANTOUR

Vallon de Salèse

N

0   1 km

car park Ⓟ

Ⓢ🄵

to Le Boréon

STAGE 1
Vallon de Salèse to Rifugio Questa

Walking Time	5hr (6hr from Le Boréon)
Difficulty	Grade 3
Distance	12.1km/7.5 miles
Ascent/Descent	1269m/546m

This stage visits Lac Nègre, one of the Mercantour's most renowned lakes and its largest, before crossing via a panoramic pass where families of ibex hang out. The little-frequented descent path is rough going, not to mention steep, and could be tricky with hard snow, which is not uncommon at the start of the summer. This is the section that earns the stage its Grade 3 rating in difficulty. Day's end is a spartan hut, but the divine setting – and delicious hearty soups – make up for any crowding or discomfort.

From the traffic barrier and **car park** in Vallon de Salèse (1665m), take the clear path marked 'Les Adus par Salèse'. In shady woodland WNW, it follows the R side of the stream at first through masses of bilberry and alpenrose shrubs. During the gentle ascent a dirt road is touched on, then joined higher up beneath a steep eroded crest. It's a short stroll R to a broad saddle

1hr – Col de Salèse (2031m). Here ignore the popular path L for Lac des Adus, and stay on the main track in gentle descent to nearby P268 (1900m) and a strategic fork R. In common with a 4WD track, you head N up a shallow side-valley with cascading streams, through light woodland, as far as the ruins of L'Agnellière (2053m) shepherds' hut.

Here a path breaks off from the track, continuing in a steady climb to **Camp Soubran** and the P270 junction (1hr, 2270m), where the return route from Fremamorta comes in. Looming almost overhead is sharply pointed Caire Pounchu. This is rounded on the final uphill section on a broad track to

1hr 15min – Lac Nègre (2354m). Indisputably blue, rather than black as the name suggests, this huge lake is justifiably popular with day walkers, who indulge in picnics and dips. Ahead, attractive rock needles stand out on the horizon, flanking your next destination.

Lac Nègre

The path continues along the R bank of the lake and over pink granite outcrops. The climb is problem-free on a perfectly graded path, past tiny tarns and rock faces where bright violets bloom. ▸

The crest above resembles a crazy rock castle from this angle.

1hr – Pas de Préfouns (2615m). Funnily enough, the name derives from the Piemontese dialect for 'precipice'! The col opens up between Testa di Tablasses and a bizarre rock monolith. Exceptionally fine views can be enjoyed back S over the Mercantour. On the Italian side the marvellous granite towers of the Cresta Savoia loom over stark Vallone di Préfouns at your feet. A long-abandoned concrete bunker is tucked into the mountainside.

Dig in your heels for the steep plunge – initially 100m of tight zigzags down a gully with faint red waymarks. As the valley begins to widen, long decent stretches of path move L across a vast basin (with chamois). This is

Looking back up to Pas de Préfouns

followed by tiring cairn-guided clambers over extensive rock falls to where the path resumes clearly on the L flank of the valley up against the cliffs, high above the valley floor. Alpenrose appears as the path winds down overlooking a transparent tarn. Bearing L further down, it joins the former game track at a **2200m junction** (1hr 15min) with marvellous views over Piano di Valasco dominated by Monte Matto.

Turn L and 15min on is a strategic fork, where you go L for a final short climb to the shores of tranquil, greeny blue Lago delle Portette and

1hr 45min – Rifugio Questa (2388m). CAI ☎ (39) 0171 97338 sleeps 20, open 1 June to 15 September www.rifugioquesta.it. Erected in 1925, this solar-powered hut was named after a mountaineer from Genova, though the name *questa* actually means 'this' in Italian. A spartan but friendly place, which can get busy especially at weekends, when overflow guests are put up in a tent. The multi-course dinner is served in shifts, as the dining area is small. Toilet and washing facilities are basic – count on having to use that corrugated iron shelter, the 'loo with a view'.

STAGE 2
Rifugio Questa to Vallon de Salèse

Walking Time	5hr 30min (6hr 20min to Le Boréon)
Difficulty	Grade 2
Distance	16km/10 miles
Ascent/Descent	569m/1292m

A superb traverse on old game tracks and paths that lead back into France via a stunningly beautiful and photogenic series of Alpine lakes. No particular difficulty is encountered in good conditions, though it is important to take into account the length of the stage.

The Fremamorta lakes in early summer

From **Rifugio Questa** (2388m) return downhill to the wide track where you turn R (E). This means a stunning, level walk, with beautiful views across to Valrossa and over Piano di Valasco, dominated at its SW extremity by pyramidal Testa del Claus. ▶ Ignore the Préfouns turn-off; further on after a rock outcrop is **Val Morta junction** (45min, 2125m).

Chamois are easily spotted on the rocky flanks amidst larch and alpenrose shrubs.

Fork R (SE) for the winding climb on another former hunting track – in excellent condition – through stark rock surroundings coloured by rare pink flowers of thrift. Testa di Tablasses dominates SW. Via a succession of natural terraces, the pass is easily gained.

1hr 30min – Colletto del Valasco (2429m). A brilliant spot. Glittering lakes nestle in glacially formed rock basins below, while the game track winds away towards distant mountains – like a 'Great Wall' of the Maritimes!

It's a leisurely stroll SSE down to the first lake, **Lago inferiore di Fremamorta** (2359m). The name is linked to a long lost episode concerning a 'dead woman'. Towering overhead are the Testa di Bresses peaks. However, you're more likely to be distracted by the sight of the magnificent Argentera massif rearing E. Derelict military buildings are scattered around, as are scented pinks and adenostyle flowers.

A rock corridor leads past the roundish middle lake (Lago mediano, 2380m) below a ridge where the red metal hut Bivacco Guiglia perches (beds for nine and cooking equipment – own stove and water necessary). Beautiful **Lago superiore** (2371m, 30min) is close at hand, with its sizeable Italian army buildings, long abandoned. ▶

For the exit to Vallone del Gesso della Valletta see Walk 14.

Easy bends climb SSW to a broad 2604m saddle in the vicinity of low-profile barracks at the foot of Cima di Fremamorta. The views are simply breathtaking, and range from the Mediterranean and the Côte d'Azur, and back to the Cuneo plain N. Go L past a tiny hut to

1hr 30min – Colle di Fremamorta (2615m) on the Franco–Italian border. Wildflowers abound – king-of-the-Alps and lilac penny-cress stand out amidst light-coloured rock.

A leisurely descent S then W, in innumerable wide curves studded with bulbous gentians, reaches a vast undulating amphitheatre housing the Lacs de Frémamorte, backed by Caire de Rogué. Amidst mountainsides dotted with alpenrose shrubs is the last lake and **Camp Soubran** (2270m, 1hr) with the P270 junction.

The winding game track, the 'Great Wall' of the Maritimes

Turn L downhill here to retrace the route taken in Stage 1 via **Col de Salèse** (2031m, 45min), and proceed downhill for the **car park** in Vallon de Salèse (1665m. 1hr 30min).

WALK 12
The Alpi Marittime Trek

Walking Time	32hr 30min or 7 days
Difficulty	Grade 2–3
Distance	67.2km/41.4 miles
Ascent/Descent	5080m/4878m
Start/Finish	Sant'Anna di Valdieri/San Giacomo
Access	A minor road branches SW from Borgo San Dalmazzo to run up Valle Gesso to Sant'Anna di Valdieri. It can also be reached by summer bus from Cuneo. At walk's end, San Giacomo, a midsummer shuttle runs to Entracque, which in turn is served by buses to Cuneo year-round. It is also possible to link back to Sant'Anna di Valdieri by public transport if you've left your car there.

A brilliant week-long meander across the Parco delle Alpi Marittime, the Italian side of the Maritime Alps, this magnificent high-altitude route sees few other walkers. A complete holiday in itself, it swings SE across breathtaking valleys touching on the unmissable highlights of this region.

Each stage concludes at a rifugio with meals and accommodation. The route is open to numerous variants, as every overnight stop has an access/exit route to a valley.

A good fitness level is recommended to ensure the long days are enjoyable and not a marathon! At a pinch, Stages 4 and 5 can be combined if time is tight. Most of the route rates Grade 2 on the difficulty scale, suitable for average walkers. Exceptions come in Stage 2 and Stage 6, but both are easily detoured – see the advice below.

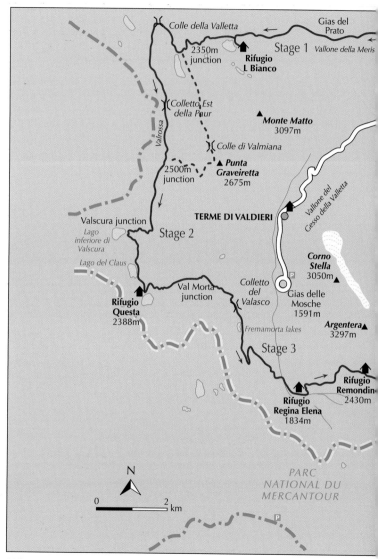

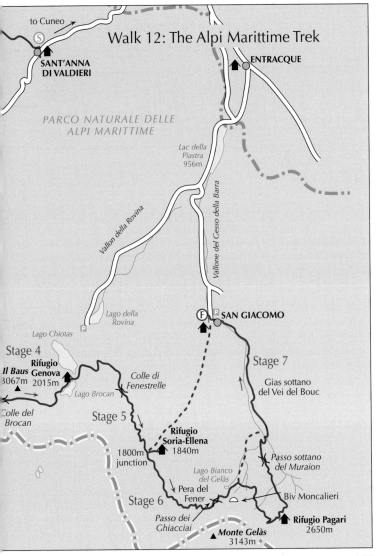

Walk 12: The Alpi Marittime Trek

to Cuneo

SANT'ANNA
DI VALDIERI

ENTRACQUE

*PARCO NATURALE DELLE
ALPI MARITTIME*

Lac della
Piastra
956m

Vallon della Rovina

Vallone del Cesso della Barra

Lago della
Rovina

SAN GIACOMO

Lago Chiotas

Stage 4

Il Baus
3067m

Rifugio
Genova
2015m

*Colle di
Fenestrelle*

Stage 7

Gias sottano
del Vei del Bouc

Lago Brocan

Stage 5

Colle del
Brocan

Rifugio
Soria-Ellena
1840m

1800m
junction

*Passo sottano
del Muraion*

Lago Bianco
del Gelàs

Biv Moncalieri

Stage 6

Pera del
Fener

Passo dei
Ghiacciai

Monte Gelàs
3143m

Rifugio Pagari
2650m

137

STAGE 1
Sant'Anna di Valdieri to Rifugio L Bianco

Walking Time	2hr 40min
Difficulty	Grade 2
Distance	7.5km/4.6 miles
Ascent	899m

This lovely varied stage makes for easy enjoyable walking. Shady wood-land characterises the initial half; thereafter Vallone de la Meris opens up, and hosts of soaring peaks come into range. The broad path, still paved in stretches, was one of the royal hunting tracks constructed at the king's behest in the 1860s. This is a guarantee of a decent gradient, as built-up curves take the sting out of the steepness. En route walkers may encounter Rifugio Bianco's guardian, who negotiates the track regularly in his ATV (all terrain vehicle) on the interminable quest for supplies to feed hungry guests.

The charming traditional village of Sant'Anna di Valdieri has grocery shops, a guest house with an excellent restaurant – **Albergo Balma Meris** ☎ (39) 0171 977832 (takes credit cards) – as well as B&B **Ciaburna dei Ribota** ☎ (39) 0171 977839 or mobile (39) 349 2915839. Separating the two estab-lishments is a wall emblazoned with 'W La Regina' ('long live the queen'), left over from the days when the royal family took flight from the summer heat on the Po plain and holidayed here.

In the upper part of **Sant'Anna di Valdieri** (1011m), alongside the fancy post office, a signpost for Vallone della Meris points walkers NW on a narrow road past the hotel and B&B.

The way climbs steeply past tiny old houses half-built into the rock face and sporting protruding balconies. The village is left behind for cool shady mountain ash and beech. Rio Meris crashes and cascades below in the deep-cut V valley, its precipitous flanks cloaked dark green.

At derelict huts Tetti Paladin (1326m) is a signed detour L to nearby Fonte Re (deliciously cool drinking water and inviting river pools). The paved mule track proceeds due W, emerging all of a sudden into a broad dry grassy basin, home to marmots, grasshoppers and aromatic Mediterranean herbs. **Gias del Prato** (1529m, 1hr 20min) marks the halfway mark. Due S rise the imposing shapes of Rocca Arculon and Punta della Merà. The going gets easier as the broad path proceeds up Vallone della Meris, the river closer now.

Past a cluster of former hunters' huts (Gias del Chiot della Sella, 1700m) are lovely rock pools. Due S rises Punta della Meris. A bridge takes you L (S) over the stream draining from Lago sottana della Sella. In the late 1800s Queen Elena (consort of King Emanuele III) would ride up here, as she loved angling for trout. The tumbledown hut next to the bridge was her boat-house. Fishing is still popular on the lake, although people who are not members of the royal family require a permit.

Lago sottano della Sella reflects the imposing rock barrier

It's not far around to beautifully positioned

2hr 40min – Rifugio L Bianco (1910m), CAI ☎ (39) 0171 97328 sleeps 60, open 15 June to 15 September www. rifugioliviobianco.it. Solar panels generally guarantee hot showers. The building was named in memory of a Second World War partisan leader. The hut's terrace is great for appreciating this vast amphitheatre and the wonderful semicircular barrier of grey peaks in upper Vallone della Meris, including a decent glimpse of Monte Matto SSE.

STAGE 2
Rifugio L Bianco to Rifugio Questa

Walking Time	7hr 20min
Difficulty	Grade 2–3
Distance	15km/9.3 miles
Ascent/Descent	1144m/666m

This extra-long but spectacular stage across to Vallone di Valasco calls for an early start. A sequence of terraces, lakes and old game tracks lead to the 'top of the world' – well, what feels like the top of the Maritimes anyway. A rugged pass gives way to a steep clamber over fallen rocks – the one and only potentially troublesome section. Low cloud or mist would make this quite tricky, indeed dangerous, as the rare markings would be hard to see. A more straightforward path with similar timing uses Colle di Valmiana, and can be used as an alternative – see below.

From **Rifugio L Bianco** (1910m) return to the bridge and fork L (W) at the tumbledown hut. A delightful path-cum-old game track climbs steadily above the glittering lake, across massive slabs of smoothed and grooved rock in this vast amphitheatre. Peeking over the upper barrier are the needle-like points belonging to Rocca la Paur and its neighbours. Marmot colonies are numerous along the way, though the arrival of walkers will send the animals scuttling to their burrows.

Interminable zigzags reinforced with dry-stone edging lead through marshy zones with a wealth of purple orchids and cotton grass. At 2121m is lone Gias Gros, a 'witty' name for a mere dot awash in a sea of nettle and dock. A few more curves uphill is the **2350m junction** (1hr 20min), where the variant forks L.

Colle di Valmiana Variant

Stepping-stones cross a gushing stream issuing from Lago soprano della Sella (out of sight). The path ascends gently SSE in the shadow of dramatic pointed L'Innominata. Not far along you descend a little across an awesome desolate basin of crumbly red rock. Near a stone shelter left by the king's hunters (2433m), ignore the fork L for Monte Matto, and keep on the seemingly neverending bends through this stone desert dominated by jagged Rocca di Valmiana W. A level stretch and an old military building precede Colle di Valmiana (2hr 10min, 2922m), where a glorious vista opens up onto the Argentera.

The path continues winding S alongside a prominent crest that culminates in Punta Graveiretta. It then swings down towards Vallone di Valmiana, past an exit route (2500m fork) for Piano di Valasco. Continue W uphill to gain Passo di Costa Miana (2620m), then it's NW to the 2500m junction (1hr 30min) at the opening of Valrossa and the main route.

Keep R for the attractive expanse of Lago soprano della Sella (2329m). The path, still a recognisable mule track, heads NE up a pretty valley with marshy lakes and chamois.

2hr – Colle della Valletta (2488m) has a vast outlook that includes Lago soprano della Valletta in a steep-sided depression at your feet, surrounded by stark red-grey walls.

Ignore the fork for Aisone, and stick to the game track as it veers L (S) in descent past tarns at the foot of Rocca

En route to Colletto Est della Paur

Pertusa and Rocca Pan Perdu. With the exception of the odd clump of grass, pink thrift and pretty light-blue endemic violets that peek out of crannies, it's all rock here. Easy curves lead up to an astoundingly scenic ridge. Tight zigzags up desolate red rock reach the 2800m mark, where the path peters out. Yellow paint stripes indicate the short clamber SW to the notch just below Rocca La Paur, namely

1hr 40min – Colletto Est della Paur (2890m). While the name is related to 'fear inducing', in this context it describes a harsh arid place that's tough to get to! Ibex laze around on the rocks, but are so well camouflaged they easily go unnoticed. The profile of their horns against the sky is a giveaway. Great views S on the other side of the pass open up with plunging Valrossa dominated by Rocca di Valmiana (SE), while the French Alps stretch out W.

Following the markings, make your way with great care down the chaos of fallen broken rock. After some 300m in descent and an hour of bashed knees – and hopefully no twisted ankles – you reach the 'idyllic' shore of the first of the lakes (2600m), befitting picnics. A faint path drops to more lakes, then an important **2500m junction** (1hr 20min), where the route from Colle di Valmiana joins up.

Turn R for a restful level stretch on the old paved game track above deep Vallone di Valasco. Below is the renovated *casa di caccia* – also known as Rifugio Valasco – and SE is the awesome Argentera at last, a light-hued massif reminiscent of the Civetta in the Italian Dolomites, and the highest mountain in the Maritime Alps. A tiny tarn marks the start of a zigzag ascent and a traverse W to

2hr 30min – Valscura junction (2245m). Unless you opt for the exit route L to Piano di Valasco (see Walk 13), turn R uphill on the old military track past skeletal buildings to **Lago inferiore di Valscura** (2274m). This wonderful spot in the shadow of Testa Malinvern (from 'bad rock') is the start of a superb stretch of bridle track, upgraded under

The king's track in upper Valscura

Evidently the king would have himself driven along in a carriage; nowadays the Rifugio Questa guardian braves the bends on his battered trail bike to transport supplies for his guests.

the fascist regime in the early 1930s. ◀ It snakes its paved way S amidst chaotic boulders of light-coloured granite, the carved initials of its constructors featuring on prominent rocks.

Beautiful **Lago del Claus** (2344m) and its islands are encountered in the shadow of monumental Testa di Claus (SW). This place name has no connection with the well-known Yuletide character sporting a white beard, but derives instead from 'closed stony place at a valley head'. After a rocky shoulder you come to a key junction – fork R (SSW) for the short climb to the unbeatable spot occupied by

1hr 10min – Rifugio Questa (2388m) on the shore of Lago delle Portette. CAI ☎ (39) 0171 97338 sleeps 20, open 15 June to 15 September, solar-heated shower www.rifugio-questa.it. This spartan but friendly place gets busy at weekends, and overflow guests are put up in a tent. A highlight of the generous dinner, which is served in shifts, is a delicious warming pulse and vegetable soup. Washing facilities consist of a tiny inside loo and hand basin, and the same outside (yes, it's that rickety corrugated-iron shack you eyed suspiciously on arrival). Erected in 1925, the hut was named after a mountaineer from Genova, though the name literally means 'this' in Italian.

STAGE 3
Rifugio Questa to Rifugio Remondino

Walking Time	6hr 10min
Difficulty	Grade 2
Distance	12.3km/7.6 miles
Ascent/Descent	952m/910m

A memorable day's walking on wide old tracks in a rollercoaster sequence across minor cols – and past pretty Laghi di Fremamorta, one of the top spots from which to admire the Argentera. (A link can be made here with Walk 11 for a detour into France.) Vallone del Gesso della Valletta is traversed and a cosy hut touched on. A climb to magnificently situated Rifugio Remondino, a hot spot for climbers on the Maritime's top summit, concludes the stage's efforts.

From **Rifugio Questa** (2388m) go back down to the key junction on the king's track and turn R (E) for a stunning level walk with beautiful views over Piano di Valasco. ▸ The Vallone del Prefouns turn-off is passed, and after a towering rock outcrop is the **Val Morta junction** (2125m, 40min). The name possibly derives from 'dead', in terms of poor terrain for grazing.

Unless you decide to exit to Terme di Valdieri (see Walk 13), turn R (SE). This is a steady ascent on another broad track that climbs through natural terraces at the foot of Cima di Valcuca. The open valley has stark rock surroundings, but is coloured by hardy wildflowers, such as pink thrift. Dominating SW are Punta di Prefouns and Testa di Tablasses.

Chamois frequent the rocky slopes amid larch and alpenrose shrubs.

145

The game track and Lago inferiore di Fremamorta

1hr 30min – Colletto del Valasco (2429m). This wonderful spot looks down to glittering lakes nestling in shallow, glacially formed basins below, while the game track winds away in the distance like a 'Great Wall' of the Maritimes!

Stroll SSE to **Lago inferiore di Fremamorta** (2359m, 10min), named after a long-forgotten 'dead woman'. Towering overhead are the Testa di Bresses peaks, but you are more likely to be distracted by the sight of the magnificent Argentera massif rearing E. A rock corridor leads past the middle lake (Lago mediano, 2380m). On the ridge above is the red metal hut Bivacco Guiglia (sleeps nine). Close at hand is

40min – Lago superiore (2371m), overlooked by old barracks and spreads of scented pinks. There are exceptional views to the Argentera and its neighbour Madre di Dio, as well as up to Cima Fremamorta SSW and its saddle (the traverse into France is described in Walk 11).

Above the water level at 2402m, turn sharp L for the clear – and wonderfully scenic – path initially due N. It veers R (SE), with increasing vegetation cover in the shape of alpenrose and grass. Some way down, after a prominent outcrop, you look out over an abandoned pasture and soon fork L down past ruined huts. A steep tract with occasional crumbly sections descends quickly to the path from Col di Ciliegia. ▶

A rustic arrow points R (E) for Rifugio Regina Elena. The faint path with white markings leads across the rocky bed of a stream, and through a thin spread of larch to

2hr – Rifugio Regina Elena (1834m), so-named in memory of Queen Elena. ☎ (39) 0171 97559 sleeps 14, open 15 June to 15 September, hot shower. A tiny, basic, but welcoming hut run by volunteer retired members of ANA, the Italian Association of Alpine Troops. Given at least one day's warning, they'll prepare meals, and any leftovers will promptly be demolished by the resident stoat.

To continue directly to Pian della Casa del Re and exit to the Terme di Valdieri, turn L (N) to join the rough road at 1735m – see Walks 9 and 14.

Rifugio Remondino

Take the faint path that drops N to cross the stream and loop up to join the main access path for Rifugio Remondino by turning R (E). It gains ground easily, amidst banks of juniper and alpenrose beneath larch trees where both marmot and chamois abound. The hut can be seen dizzily above your head at the foot of Cima di Nasta (named after its 'spear' shape). The stream is never far away, and is crossed.

Ignore the fork for Colle di Mercantour, and back on the L bank of the watercourse continue steadily upwards, curving into Vallone Assedras under towering Madre di Dio and Cima di Cessole. On stone steps brightened by adenostyle flowers, the path circles beneath the hut's outcrop perch, finally reaching

En route to Colle del Brocan

2hr – Rifugio Remondino (2430m). CAI ☎ (39) 0171 97327 sleeps 50, open 15 June to 15 September, hot shower. Comfortable, spacious establishment with plenty of windows for enjoying the views. It's usually crawling with climbers and overflowing with mountaineering gear due to the vicinity of the Argentera. The vast outlook includes the rocky ridges above the Fremamorta lakes, while of course above, due E, is Cima di Nasta, flanked by Cima Paganini and Il Bastione, without forgetting the Argentera Sud NE, and closer at hand due S, Catena del CAI.

STAGE 4

Rifugio Remondino to Rifugio Genova

Walking Time	4hr
Difficulty	Grade 2–3
Distance	4.4km/2.7 miles
Ascent/Descent	462m/877m

A magnificent and highly rewarding day spent on a high-altitude route where panoramas stretch to the Ecrins region of the French Alps, Monviso, not to mention closer at hand the Maritime Alps themselves. Once snow has melted away, paths are clear and offer no special difficulty, apart from a rather steep descent from the pass. Flora buffs should keep their eyes peeled during the ascent, as the ancient king saxifrage grows on the west-facing rock faces above the hut.

Fit walkers can combine Stages 4 and 5, continuing on to Rifugio Soria-Ellena – a total of 7hr.

From **Rifugio Remondino** (2430m) the faint path for Colle del Brocan is shown by painted marks on rocks. At the foot of Catena del CAI, it's ESE across crumbly rock following red/yellow marks. A little clambering is required

Soon a branch L leads through to Lago di Nasta – see Walk 16.

over smooth rock slabs and up a gully that gives access to a rough desolate basin where, remarkably, jewel-like white-green saxifrage grows on bare surfaces. ▶

The panoramas are simply astounding, but there is still room for improvement! The climb continues S without respite, cutting across rocky terrain that is home to endemic violets under Il Bastione. In good conditions even the Mediterranean can be seen from this marvellous vantage point.

1hr 40min – Colle del Brocan (2892m) a notch separating Il Bastione and Cima di Brocan. The apt name derives from 'jagged point' and 'broken rocks'. The much-coveted (and protected) genipi grows up here, while ibex rest on impossible perches, keeping an eye on walkers.

Brace yourself for the ensuing plunge down a chaotic rubble funnel due E, guided by showy painted yellow waymarks, through a scooped-out cirque where snow lies late. Watch your step on the loose stones. Il Baus stands out N, a magnet for climbers, while below are the pretty blue expanses of Lago Brocan and Chiotas.

Lago Brocan has shrunk in size over recent years, but it still attracts large numbers of visitors to sunbathe here. Wheeling alpine choughs abound too, ever hopeful for picnic scraps.

Over the lip, the path improves, crossing grass and glacially smoothed slabs, where flowers sprout between rocks. Monte Gelàs is glimpsed briefly SE, while further afield N beyond the Piastra dam is a landmark limestone ridge beyond Entracque. Ahead E rises majestic Cima Ciamberlane. ◀

At the base of Vallone del Brocan on the northern tip of the lake stands

2hr 20min – Rifugio Genova (2015m) ☎ (39) 0171 978138, CAI, sleeps 60, open 15 June to 15 September, hot shower, credit cards www.rifugiogenova.it. The comfortable modern building was donated by the Electricity Commission to replace the 1898 hut, the very first of its kind in the Maritimes, submerged when the lake was dammed in the 1970s. It was named in honour of the Genoese branch of the Italian Alpine Club, who initiated the endeavour.

STAGE 5
Rifugio Genova to Rifugio Soria-Ellena

Walking Time	3hr
Difficulty	Grade 2
Distance	8km/4.9 miles
Ascent/Descent	493m/668m

In common with Walk 9, this enjoyable straightforward crossing leads to Vallone del Gesso della Barra and its hospitable rifugio. As Stage 6 entails considerable difficulty, less experienced walkers can opt out after the descent from Colle di Fenestrelle and conclude the trek at San Giacomo – see below.

Leave **Rifugio Genova** (2015m) by way of the dirt road circling Lago Chiotas (also called Bacino artificiale del Chiotas). Some 15min along, a marked path forks R at 2010m for the climb to the next pass. ▸

For the exit route to Lago della Rovina – 1hr 30min – continue around the dam wall as for Walk 9, Stage 3.

Initially E amidst shrub vegetation and wildflowers, the old game route ascends Vallone di Fenestrelle, dominated by Roc di Fenestrelle SSE. In a vast semicircle surmounted by the imposing barrier of Rocce di Laura, innumerable hairpin bends take the sting out of the ascent. A final stretch S leads across rainbow-coloured rock and past the twin tarns that precede

1hr 30min – Colle di Fenestrelle (2463m), summer home of surprising numbers of ibex.

The 600m descent proceeds SSE in restful zigzags under Punta delle Lobbie, making its straightforward way downhill, cutting across vast grassy slopes where herds of chamois feed. Soon after the ruins of a herder's hut, Gias Alvé, you finally reach a huge boulder and **1800m junction** on Piano del Praiet. Here it is feasible to exit the trek by heading valleywards to San Giacomo, as follows.

Exit to San Giacomo (1hr 45min)
Turn L (NNE) on the stony 4WD track that descends Vallon del Gesso della Barra, with the odd short-cut. There are plenty of opportunities for admiring Monte Gelàs SSE and Ray della Siula. The rushing torrent carrying snow-melt from upper snowfields is approached, then a clearing where a sign commemorates the wartime flight of Jewish refugees from France. Then the onset of thick beech woods covering the lower mountainsides announces that the hamlet of San Giacomo (1213m) is not far off – see Stage 7 for details of facilities.

However, before that well-earned cool beer can be enjoyed, a last (short) uphill leg awaits to

1hr 40min – Rifugio Soria-Ellena (1840m). ☎ (39) 0171 978382, CAI, sleeps 62, open 15 June to 15 September, hot shower www.rifugiosoriaellena.com. A welcoming establishment, if a little cramped, where you'll be splendidly fed. Bird lovers will be interested to know that this is the haunt of the awesome lammergeier, or bearded vulture, which has been re-introduced with great success.

The lakeside track from Rifugio Genova

Almost directly overhead SE is Gelàs, the 'Mont Blanc of the Maritimes', whose 3142m peak was first scaled in far-off 1864 by a team of aristocrats led by Paolo di Saint-Robert. The name derives from 'icy conditions', but it also means 'curse' in the vernacular. A story recounts that it was once the verdant home of three beautiful sisters, who were subjected to the unseemly attentions of men from Entracque. The maidens met a violent end, and in empathy the mountain mutated into an icy waste. The name Gelàs has also been used for a liquor made with bitter herbs that reputedly aids digestion.

STAGE 6

Rifugio Soria-Ellena to Rifugio Pagari

Walking Time	6hr
Difficulty	Grade 3+
Distance	9km/5.5 miles
Ascent/Descent	1130m/320m

This is the most difficult stage of the whole trek, with an especially steep valley with loose terrain to be negotiated, followed by a tricky if short ice/snow passage preceding Passo dei Ghiacciai. Do check on its condition at the rifugio before starting out (crampons may be recommended). If in any doubt at all, avoid it completely by turning valleywards and following the jeep track directly to San Giacomo – see Exit to San Giacomo, above. Rifugio Pagari can then be visited separately on Walk 18. It goes without saying that perfect weather is essential, as low cloud would make orientation difficult, and wet conditions transform the route into a dangerous undertaking.

The good news is that other walkers are few and far between on this route around the majestic Gelàs with its fossil glacier pockets. After the spectacular (and exposed) Cresta dei Ghiacciai there is a well-placed bivouac hut and a brace of pretty lakes, followed by a panoramic traverse to Rifugio Pagari.

From **Rifugio Soria-Ellena** (1840m) the 'official' route to Pera di Fener returns to the valley floor. This is a longer way but clearer after 20min S up the valley in common with the route for Colle di Finestra; you need the signed path E.

Otherwise, if you're prepared to keep your eyes peeled for occasional red waymarks on the initial 20min, it's fine to take the narrow stony path SSE from the rifugio, a slightly shorter route. Traversing rugged mountainsides, it follows a water pipe and crosses a side-stream. Heading up a rock slope green with lichen, the faint path guided by cairns bears R (S) and steeply uphill to join the main path at the 2100m mark. ◀

This area is called Gorgia della Maura, the name a reference to 'dark', possibly from the blackish rock surfaces, wet with meltwater from ice fields, which feed alpenrose and bilberry shrubs.

Next is a steady climb SE on the zigzags of the old hunting track, narrow in parts and with the occasional collapsed section and the odd stream to cross. Above is the extended outline of Cresta della Maura. Ignore the turn-offs and stick to the main path through dry desolate terrain, finally terminating at

2hr 45min – Pera del Fener (2698m) and the recognisable shape of a hunting enclosure. This used to be the base of the Ghiacciaio Nord Gelàs, but its shrunken icy body has retreated somewhat and is high above SW nowadays. The principal peak of Monte Gelàs is due S.

A sign here warns that the following itinerary is for expert walkers only. In fact the path as such all but disappears immediately. However, behind a prominent boulder are the first of the consistent red markers that point you up an abrupt slope of mobile broken rock of the 'one step forward, two steps back' variety! Luckily it's not far to an immense desert-like plateau of stone, which is relatively level and affords stunning views to the Argentera NW. ◀ Further on NE, rougher rock surfaces demand a little clambering, with the help of a cable; a little higher up is a second length of thick wire for the tricky crossing of a long tongue of snow and ice which remains hard and slippery all summer long. Take great care.

Incredibly, daisies and thrift are found up here.

154

Following red paint splashes closely, only metres above you gain

1hr 15min – Passo dei Ghiacciai (2750m) marked by a rope hung with prayer flags. It is located on a razor-sharp ridge below Cima Chafrion, which was named after a 17th-century cartographer.

After a short dip to the L, dizzy exposed Cresta dei Ghiacciai is followed N, with incredible views to triangular Monviso NNW and even glaciated Monte Rosa N, not to mention the spread of the Cuneo plain. You soon fork down R to beautifully placed **Bivacco Moncalieri** (2710m) and its many ibex, near a pocket glacier. This wood and metal structure dates back to 1983 and replaces a previous hut swept away by winter avalanches. (It can sleep nine, but users need their own cooking gear; there is water nearby).

On Cresta dei Ghiacciai

Amid parsley fern and crimson houseleek blooms, a decent path moves down NNE to **Lago Bianco del Gelàs** (2553m, 30min) beneath Punta della Siula. On the lake's edge, three-way red arrows on a large rock show the way (differing a little from the commercial maps).

Direct Exit to San Giacomo (3hr)

For a direct exit avoiding Rifugio Pagari, take the L (N) fork from here for a steep narrow path dropping via Vallone di Pantacreus and its waterfalls (see Walk 19). This rejoins the main route at 1550m (1hr 45min) and proceeds to San Giacomo – see below.

Fork R past a smaller lake to where the path crosses a stream flowing over smooth rock. In a gentle descent SE you cross grassy terrain colonised by silvery leaved adenostyle flowers. Soon after a precarious passage over a crumbly rock flank is Passo soprano del Muraion (2430m), with a landmark rock spur.

Vestiges of an old hunting track appear, and the path widens in ascent, skirting S at the foot of Caire del Muraion, an outlier of Cima della Maledia. The rifugio is soon visible, and it's straightforward walking in the company of ibex and vast views. The final stretch crosses the hut's water pipe, climbing through a small botanical garden to

1hr 30min – Rifugio Pagari (also known as Rifugio Federici-Marchesini) (2650m). ☎ (39) 0171 978398, CAI, sleeps 24, open 15 June to 15 September www.rifugiopagari.com. Located in amazing rockscapes with vast views in a spot teeming with wildlife, this eyrie is the highest manned hut in the whole of the Maritime Alps. An overnight stay here is a unique experience. It is run by an aesthete who takes great care in the preparation of healthy meals (and beer brewed on the spot!); he has been known to spend the long dark winter months here snowed-in. The hut offers little in the way of mod cons – a trifling drawback abundantly compensated by the magical setting. Glaciers on the crest linking Cima

di Pagari with Maledia reach down towards the building. (For more details, see Walk 19.)

Rifugio Pagari

STAGE 7
Rifugio Pagari to San Giacomo

Walking Time	3hr 20min
Difficulty	Grade 2
Distance	11km/6.8 miles
Descent	1437m

A beautiful valley descent on delightful paths is a relatively relaxing if lengthy way to conclude this magnificent trek. The stark ice and rock realms of upper Vallone del Muraion are followed by pastoral Vallon di Moncolomb, then dense cool beech woods. Hostel accommodation is on offer at the walk's end, though the shuttle bus option from San Giacomo terminates at Entracque and hotels.

The Foresteria at San Giacomo

From **Rifugio Pagari** (2650m) the broad path winds its way downhill NE in easy curves, soon accompanied by veritable smothers of alpenrose and juniper. Alongside R is a perfect funnel-shaped moraine left by a retreating glacier beneath the Clapier peaks, while Lago Bianco dell'Agnel is glimpsed E under the summit of the same name. At 2280m the route veers L (NW) parallel to the floor of Vallone del Muraion, gradually dropping past an abandoned shepherds' hut overgrown with nettles, to reach **Passo sottano del Muraion** (2050m), a great look-out point opposite jagged Cima del Tor.

Tree cover starts with green alder, which thrives thanks to the proximity of trickling side-streams. Past another old hut and over rock slabs the path proceeds N, gradually approaching the V of the valley floor, where rowan and laburnum provide shade alongside the cascading torrent. Soon after crossing tumbling Rio Pantacreus, where you may get wet feet, at **1550m** it is joined by the direct route from Lago Bianco del Gelàs. It's not far to a restful level tract to Gias Colomb (1444m) and the log bridge to the R riverbank in Vallone di Moncolomb and the key junction at **Gias sottano del Vei del Bouc** (1430m, 2hr 20min) where Walk 20 forks off.

A rough road leads N through flat pastures, finally descending through lovely beech woods to an old royal hunting pavilion (Casa Reale di Caccia, 1250m), now a summer holiday retreat for families. The road quickly reaches the cluster of buildings at

1hr – San Giacomo (1213m). The place name – St James – is a reminder that in medieval times this was a stopover and hospice for pilgrims heading for the renowned sanctuary of Compostella in Spain. Nowadays it is used by the faithful of Entracque, who cross Colle di Finestra in August to worship at Madone de Fenestre in France (see Walks 6 and 9).

Accommodation can be found at the **Park Foresteria** or walkers' hostel ☎ (39) 0171 978444, sleeps 20, open mid-June to mid-September, hot shower, cooking facilities. There's also a park visitor centre, café-restaurant, camping ground (**Sotto il Faggio** ☎ mobile (39) 349 7305438 open June–Sept) and summer shuttle bus to Entracque.

WALK 13
The Valasco Tour

Walking Time	7hr or 1 day
Difficulty	Grade 1–2
Distance	20.2km/12.5 miles
Ascent/Descent	1000m/1000m
Start/Finish	Terme di Valdieri
Access	Located in Valle Gesso 31km from Cuneo, the Terme are easily reached June to September by bus (from Cuneo) as well as the midsummer shuttle service via Valdieri.

Piano di Valasco and Testa di Claus

In the 1800s the glorious Piano di Valasco ('large valley') was greatly enjoyed by the hunting entourages of the Italian royal family, as it occupied the heart of the *Riserva reale di caccia*, or royal game reserve. Once the bottom of a lake, the lush elongated meadow basin was also shaped by long-gone glaciers. Dotted with spruce, gurgling streams run through it, and it is surrounded on

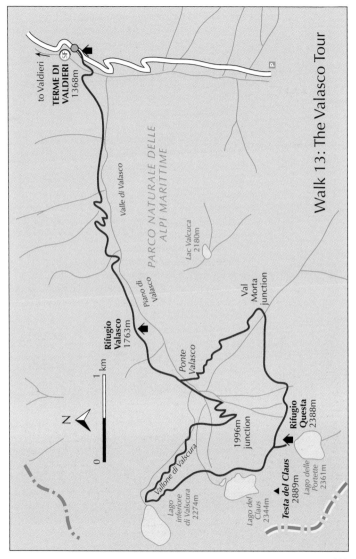

Walk 13: The Valasco Tour

to Valdieri

TERME DI VALDIERI 1368m

P

Valle di Valasco

PARCO NATURALE DELLE ALPI MARITTIME

Lac Valcuca 2180m

Piano di Valasco

Rifugio Valasco 1763m

Val Morta junction

Ponte Valasco

Rifugio Questa 2388m

1996m junction

Vallone di Valscura

Lago delle Portette 2361m

Testa del Claus 2889m

Lago inferiore di Valscura 2274m

Lago del Claus 2344m

N

0   1 km

three sides by breathtaking ridges topped by jagged pale-grey mountains. Paved tracks broad enough for carriages radiate out to penetrate neighbouring valleys; most were upgraded in the 1930s when the Italian fascist regime was reinforcing its borders. Testifying to the presence of privileged nobility is a turreted *casa di caccia* ('hunting pavilion'), 'a square of buildings like an Oriental *serai*', according to WM Conway in 1894. Recently renovated it is now Rifugio Valasco.

This walk is simply brilliant, although a little long for a single day, and there are hosts of inviting picnic spots along the way. Bear in mind that it can always be extended with an overnight stay at either of the two refuges. On the other hand, quite a few variants cut the distance.

Note Extensive avalanches struck the lower valley in spring 2009; the path was repaired immediately, but the tree cover has been devastated in patches and will take many years to recover.

Straddling a gushing torrent and cloaked in cool beech woods is the historic spa resort Terme di Valdieri, or '*bagni*' (baths), where the walk starts. Discovered long ago by the ancient Romans, the springs became fashionable with royalty in the days when Italy had a king (see the Introduction for more on this). Accommodation is at the cavernous Hotel Royal, which also runs the *posto tappa*. Otherwise there's family-style Hotel Turismo. A park visitor centre and extensive botanical garden complete the picture.

WALK

Past the visitor centre and turn-off for the Giardino Botanico in the upper part of **Terme di Valdieri** (1390m), take the wide track W in common with the GTA route and red/white waymarks. After the chapel of San Giovanni, at the first bend a short-cut can be taken, leading alongside a delightful succession of cascades in light mixed woodland. It picks up the main track on the last leg climbing steeply to emerge on **Piano di Valasco** (1763m, 1hr 10min). This beautiful flat pasture-cum-peat bog boasts a brilliant array of flowers. Ahead SW the imposing

*The track zigzags up
Vallone di Valscura*

pyramid of Testa del Claus, just one in a stunning crown
of mountains, closes the valley.

Rifugio Valasco is skirted. Thereafter the track proceeds on the lower edge of woodland, to **Ponte Valasco**
(1814m) over a waterfall (the return route slots in here
later). Without crossing this bridge, turn R (SW) on a path
across the upper basin. The track is joined once again
amidst thinning larches and rowan as it winds uphill to
a prominent stunted larch and **1996m junction** (a shorter
direct route to Rifugio Questa forks SSW here).

Continuing N you cross gushing streams, climbing
steadily towards a deep-red rock face, then a short tunnel leads NW into Vallone di Valscura. A series of curves
via a gully amidst glacially smoothed rock passes old
military buildings, reaching **Lago inferiore di Valscura**
(2274m, 2hr). This wonderful spot in the shadow of Testa
Malinvern (from 'bad rock') is the start of one of the best
stretches of bridle track in the whole of the Maritimes.
In remarkable contrast to the former king being driven
along in a carriage, nowadays the Rifugio Questa guardian braves the bends on his battered trail bike.

So, in common with Walk 12 and the GTA, turn L
(S) to follow the route snaking its way through granite
boulders; keen eyes will spot the initials of its constructors carved on prominent rocks. En route is beautiful

Lago del Claus (2344m) and its tiny islands shaded by monumental Testa di Claus (SW), no connection with the well-known Yuletide character, as the place name derives instead from 'closed stony place at a valley head'.

After a rocky shoulder is a key junction where you fork R (SSW) for the short climb to the unbeatable spot occupied by **Rifugio Questa** (2388m, 1hr 10min). A spartan but friendly place, it gets very busy on weekends. See Walk 11 for more details.

The hut stands on the shore of Lago delle Portette, the name refering to 'mountain pass, small aperture in a crest'. High above, SE, are the rock needle profiles of the Cresta Savoia, named after the prince and princesses who were the children of the Italian king Vittorio Emanuele III: Maria, Giovanna, Mafalda, Umberto and Jolanda.

Go back down to the key junction and turn R for a stunning, level walk with beautiful views across to Valrossa and over Piano di Valasco. ◄ Pass the Préfouns valley turn-off and round a rock outcrop to the **Val Morta junction** (2125m). Here turn L on a narrower but clear path NW, which meanders down to **Ponte Valasco** (1814m, 1hr 10min).

Chamois hang out on these rocky flanks where larch and alpenrose shrubs prosper.

Now it's a matter of retracing the route followed earlier on, to end this memorable route at **Terme di Valdieri** (1390m, 1hr 30min).

Hotel Royal ☎ (39) 0171 97106 sleeps 178, open June to late September www.termedivaldieri.it. *Posto tappa* accommodation: sleeps 24, open 15 June to 15 September, hot shower, meals at the hotel.

Hotel Turismo ☎ (39) 0171 97334, open end April to September.

Rifugio Valasco ☎ (39) 348 3230266, sleeps 45, open 15 June to 15 September and some weekends www.rifugiovalasco.it.

Rifugio Questa CAI ☎ (39) 0171 97338 sleeps 20, open 15 June to 15 September, solar-heated shower www.rifugioquesta.it. (See Walk 11 for more details.)

WALK 14

The Fremamorta Loop

Walking Time	5hr 20min or 1 day
Difficulty	Grade 2
Distance	12.2km/7.5 miles
Ascent/Descent	811m/811m
Start/Finish	Gias delle Mosche
Access	Vallone del Gesso della Valletta, accessible from Terme di Valdieri, is of key importance for the Argentera. Cars are allowed 3km up as far as the Gias delle Mosche parking area. If on foot allow 50min to here, and 40min for the return – an extra 1hr 30min in all.

Unquestionably the most photogenic lakes in this part of the world, the divine Laghi di Fremamorta occupy an ancient glacially formed trough that runs parallel to the valley floor. Another feature of this memorable circular walk is a wonderful stretch of the 'king's highway', a superb broad stone track that snakes its way o'er ridge and vale. To top it off, the vantage point of the lakes is renowned as a lookout par excellence onto the mighty Argentera massif, the 'monarch of the Maritimes' with its collection of 3000m-plus peaks. What more could be asked of a walk?

To extend the pleasure over two days, by all means overnight at Rifugio Regina Elena, a cosy if small hut on the valley floor. Otherwise walkers equipped with sleeping bag, food and cooking kit can overnight at stunningly located Bivacco Guiglia.

WALK

Leave **Gias delle Mosche** (1591m) on the signed path branching off the road R (initially N), past a ruined hut and across a bridge. Spreads of alpenrose and larch trees thin gradually as the clear path veers W, gaining height quickly thanks to well-graded zigzags up rocky flanks where shy, fleet-footed chamois hang out. A panoramic outcrop at 1960m is a chance to get your breath back

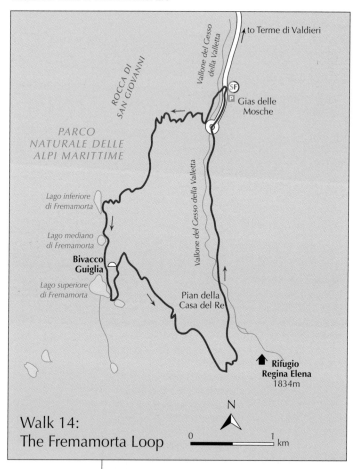

PARCO
NATURALE DELLE
ALPI MARITTIME

ROCCA DI
SAN GIOVANNI

Vallone del Gesso della Valletta

to Terme di Valdieri

SF
P

Gias delle
Mosche

Vallone del Gesso della Valletta

Lago inferiore
di Fremamorta

Lago mediano
di Fremamorta

**Bivacco
Guiglia**

Lago superiore
di Fremamorta

Pian della
Casa del Re

**Rifugio
Regina Elena**
1834m

N

Walk 14:
The Fremamorta Loop

0   1 km

while admiring the valley extending to Colle Mercantour
and Col de Cerise on the French border.

The ensuing traverse S at the foot of Rocca di San
Giovanni means ever-improving views to the bulky
Argentera massif due E and the imposing Madre di Dio
ridge. Small streams are easily crossed, as is a rock

barrier, giving access to **Lago inferiore di Fremamorta** (2359m, 2hr 30min). The twin Bresses peaks dominate the rock corridor, which is dotted with military odds and ends, not to mention scented patches of pinks.

The Argentera from the Fremamorta track

Turn L (S) onto the former game track for the gentle ascent to the hollow holding the next lake (Lago mediano, 2380m). The trail is soon flanked on the L by a ridge, where a short detour can be made to **Bivacco Guiglia** (2421m), a bright-red metal hut with a stupendous view.

Close at hand is ravishing **Lago superiore** (2371m, 30min), with its spacious Italian army barracks, long abandoned. From the path junction here (where Walk 11 heads over into France via Colle di Fremamorta), turn sharp L (N). A superbly scenic path leads across a vast glacially smoothed rock surface, soon veering SE as grass and alpenrose appear. After rounding a prominent outcrop further down, you fork L past old huts. This becomes quite steep and narrow, though the bottom is

Old barracks at Lago superiore di Fremamorta

Rifugio Regina Elena – see Walk 12 for details.

soon reached and the Col de Cerise path joined. Unless you want to detour to Rifugio Regina Elena (see Walk 12), turn L (N) through to the rough road at **Pian della Casa del Re** (1735m, 1hr 50min).

It's a pleasant stroll along Vallone del Gesso della Valletta past the dairy farm. Marmot colonies thrive amongst the undergrowth, watched over by flashy European jays. The walk concludes at **Gias delle Mosche** (1591m, 30min). ◀

Bivacco Guiglia has bunk beds for nine.

WALK 15
Rifugio Bozano

Walking Time	4hr or 1 day
Difficulty	Grade 2
Distance	9.1km/5.6 miles
Ascent/Descent	862m/862m
Start/Finish	Gias delle Mosche
Access	See Walk 14

A splendid, unmissable walk that explores the mid-altitude belt of the westernmost face of the Argentera massif, with the loftiest peaks in the Maritime Alps. It is worth every (steep) step of the climb. The destination is Rifugio Bozano and its breathtaking setting, and includes a short loop on the return leg.

The hut stands on a prominent outcrop directly beneath the striking profile of Corno Stella, an inclined formation that stands out from the main ridge. An irresistible magnet for climbers, its SW face rises dramatically 450m here. Dubbed '*Roc inaccessible*' by Fritz Mader at the turn of the century, Corno Stella was scaled shortly afterwards in 1903 by Count Victor De Cessole with expert guides Ghigo and Plent. This success led to the construction of a hut at 2400m in 1921. This original structure is now a mountaineering museum, and a modern timber building was inaugurated in 2001, reminiscent of Noah's Ark.

The panoramic terrace ringing the refuge is ship-shaped, with a curved bow and tapered stern, and even equipped with 'lifebuoys' – well, it does belong to the Genova branch of the Alpine Club, and was named in honour of a past president. The guardian lugs provisions up the path in his rucksack on a weekly basis. It is an essential base for mountaineers attempting the myriad routes on this NW part of the Argentera.

The walk holds plenty of interest for wildlife lovers – starting with rare woodpeckers in the lower conifer

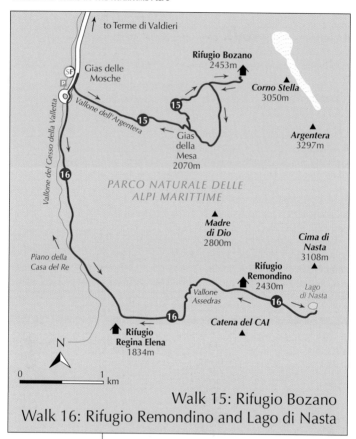

to Terme di Valdieri

Gias delle
Mosche

Rifugio Bozano
2453m

▲ **Corno Stella**
3050m

Vallone dell'Argentera

15

15

Gias
della
Mesa
2070m

▲ **Argentera**
3297m

Vallone del Cesso della Valletta

16

*PARCO NATURALE DELLE
ALPI MARITTIME*

▲ **Madre
di Dio
2800m**

**Cima di
Nasta
3108m**
▲

**Rifugio
Remondino
2430m**

*Lago
di Nasta*

*Piano della
Casa del Re*

*Vallone
Assedras*

16

16

16

Catena del CAI
▲

**Rifugio
Regina Elena
1834m**

N

0   1
├────────────────┤ km

Walk 15: Rifugio Bozano
Walk 16: Rifugio Remondino and Lago di Nasta

wood, there are sizeable herds of chamois on grazing
areas. Cheeky alpine choughs circle above the hut in the
eternal quest for easy scraps.

WALK

A tad downhill from the parking area at **Gias delle
Mosche** (1591m, 'grazing area of flies'!) is the signed
path L (E) for Rifugio Bozano via Vallone dell'Argentera. It

immediately launches into tight zigzags climbing quickly through thick conifer wood of larch, pine, fir and Arolla, with many gnarled old trees. The welcome shade gradually diminishes and you emerge on open grassland fed by a stream. Ahead the Serra dell'Argentera rises majestically, an impenetrable barrier.

Past **Gias della Mesa** (also called Mesdì – 2070m), an old grazing site where the return path slots in, you loop L (N) crossing terrain that is becoming noticeably bare. A little clambering sees you over a glacially modelled rock outcrop, then Corno Stella can be admired in all its glory. A final climb due E, and the welcoming rifugio is at last seen on its great terrace above the old hut.

Rifugio Bozano (2453m, 2hr 20min) Take plenty of time out here to take in the marvellous panorama that ranges from Corno Stella and the Argentera virtually overhead, outlier La Madre di Dio S, and across Vallone del Gesso della Valletta to the Fremamorta–Bresses line-up that extends N with Rocca soprana di San Giovanni. Quite something.

Rifugio Bozano below Corno Stella

Refreshed and inspired, return downhill on the rocky route for 20min to a minor fork marked 'Sentiero dei Pastori' ('shepherds' path') for a short variant. Red paint flashes point you L (S) over rocks to a decent if narrow path to a pasture basin beneath sheer cliffs. A stream is crossed in the vicinity of a ruined hut. Further on, fork R (NW) with yellow markers leads back across the watercourse; thereafter you make your way down to rejoin the main path at **Gias della Mesa** (2070m, 50min).

A further 50min later and you're back on the valley floor at **Gias delle Mosche** (1591m).

Rifugio Bozano ☎ (39) 0171 97351 CAI, sleeps 40, open 15 June to 15 September, hot shower www.rifugiobozano.it.

The Argentera from Gias della Mesa

WALK 16

Rifugio Remondino and Lago di Nasta

Walking Time	6hr 10min or 1 day
Difficulty	Grade 2
Distance	12.4km/7.7 miles
Ascent/Descent	1209m/1209m
Start/Finish	Gias delle Mosche
Access	See Walk 14

A tiny sparkling tarn in a forbidding cirque at 2800m is the goal of this superb walk. Set in a stark rockscape on the upper SE flanks of the Argentera massif, it can be ice-bound well into the summer months. Even if the walk is limited to Rifugio Remondino, 400m and 1hr lower down, the experience will still be well worth the effort. A hospitable modern structure buzzing with climbing talk and overflowing with gear, Rifugio Remondino has a brilliant far-reaching outlook, and does an irresistible *crostata* fruit tart.

This route is shown with Walk 15 on the map on page 170.

Both flora and fauna are high profile: after the European jays, marmots and chamois on the lower slopes, birds of prey glide above the clearings, while both ptarmigan and ibex are frequent above the hut, despite the large numbers of two-legged visitors. On the plant front, the spectacular and famed ancient king saxifrage grows on the sheer rocks high up.

The lofty Argentera massif extends in an unbroken N–S line for roughly 1km crammed with pointy crests and a host of elegant peaks over 3000m. The majestic 'monarch of the Maritimes', as described by mountaineer WM Conway in 1894, peaks at 3297m with Cima Sud, the highest point in the whole of the Maritime Alps. Memorable summit attempts include that in 1878 by a young DW Freshfield, who actually climbed nearby Cima di Nasta, mistaking it for Cima Sud. The honour – the very next year – went to the Rev WA Coolidge with his trusty

Rifugio Remondino and the Argentera

Swiss guides, Almer father and son; they followed the gruelling icy Canale di Lourousa to the north. Nowadays the most popular *via normale* takes Passo dei Detriti from Rifugio Remondino.

WALK

From **Gias delle Mosche** (1591m) follow the unsurfaced road in gentle ascent S alongside the stream in Vallone del Gesso della Valletta. ◄ The pasture on either side of the valley is enjoyed by the cows based at a nearby summer farm.

Larch, laburnum and juniper shrubs grow amidst scattered rocks where marmots frolic.

At **Piano della Casa del Re** (1743m, 30min) – 'plain of the king's house', referring to the 1800s and the royal game reserve – clear signs point you L (SSE) on a well-trodden path. This quickly gains ground, enjoying the meagre shade of the last of the conifers. The hut is visible far far above on its dizzy perch at the foot of Cima di Nasta (so-named because its 'spear' shape).

A bridge crosses the stream and before long a fork for Colle di Mercantour is ignored. Soon back on the L side of the torrent, you continue steadily upwards, curving into Vallone Assedras below the towering peaks of Madre di Dio and Cima di Cessole. Stone steps brightened by thrift, adenostyle flowers and alpine cabbage circle beneath the outcrop housing you eventually reach

Rifugio Remondino (2430m, 2hr 10min). This comfortable building replaces a 1934 bivouac hut. The vast outlook includes the rocky ridges above the Fremamorta lakes NNW, while of course above due E is Cima di Nasta, flanked by Cima Paganini and Passo dei Detriti NW.

To push on for the lake, head uphill ESE on a faint path (for Nasta/Brocan) indicated by red/yellow paint splashes on rocks at the foot of Catena del CAI. The crumbly rock that is traversed makes it a little tiring, and some clambering is required to gain smoothed rock slabs. A short gully leads onto a broad desolate shoulder, where jewel-like white-green saxifrage grows on bare surfaces. The views are stunning, reaching over the peaks well beyond Vallon del Gesso della Valletta.

Leave the path for Colle del Brocan (and Walk 12), and keep your eyes open for the faint branch L marked by the odd cairn and leading through to **Lago di Nasta** (2800m, 1hr) – a wild other-worldly spot at the foot of soaring Il Bastione and Il Baus. The semicircle of stones nearby was a hunter's stand in the days of the royal game reserve.

Return the same way to **Rifugio Remondino** and down to **Piano della Casa del Re**, then via the valley floor back to the parking area at **Gias delle Mosche** (1591m, 2hr 40min).

Rifugio Remondino CAI ☎ (39) 0171 97327 sleeps 50, open 15 June to 15 September, hot shower.

WALK 17
Vallone di Lourousa

Walking Time	6hr 40min or 1 day
Difficulty	Grade 2
Distance	14km/8.6 miles
Ascent/Descent	1158m/1158m
Start/Finish	Terme di Valdieri
Access	Located in Valle Gesso 31km from Cuneo, the Terme are easily reached by a June to September bus (from Cuneo) as well as a midsummer shuttle service.

The vast Vallone di Lourousa followed in this route gouges its way SE up the northern edge of the famous Argentera massif. Deciduous wood gives way to pasture, and then a wild rocky chaos up high where conditions border on severe. Close to the top, and the day's objective – Colle di Chiapous – stands Rifugio Morelli-Buzzi, a very popular base for climbers attempting the Argentera, and a recommended lunch venue for day walkers. The Provençal name 'Lourousa' means 'the glacier' or 'the icy summit', and was originally applied to the dramatic *canale* that breaks off halfway.

This well-trodden route is long, and quite tiring in view of the height gain and subsequent loss, but is problem-free in good conditions. The day can be shortened marginally by going only as far as the refuge, reducing the time to 5hr 20min.

The walk start, Terme di Valdieri, is an old-style spa resort that nestles in cool beech woods at the foot of precipitous Monte Matto in Valle Gesso. Facilities include a stately hotel and Swiss-style chalets dating back to the mid 1800s, when this valley was the heart of the royal game reserve. See Walk 13 for more details

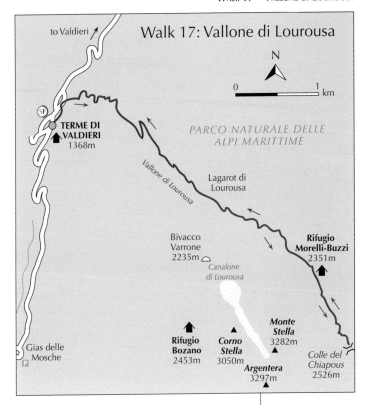

Walk 17: Vallone di Lourousa

to Valdieri

N

0   1 km

SF

**TERME DI
VALDIERI**
1368m

*PARCO NATURALE DELLE
ALPI MARITTIME*

Vallone di Lourousa

Lagarot di
Lourousa

Bivacco
Varrone
2235m

*Canalone
di Lourousa*

**Rifugio
Morelli-Buzzi**
2351m

**Rifugio
Bozano**
2453m

▲
*Corno
Stella*
3050m

*Monte
Stella*
3282m
▲

Gias delle
Mosche

Argentera
3297m
▲

*Colle del
Chiapous*
2526m

WALK

Leave **Terme di Valdieri** (1368m) by way of the car park opposite the entrance to the Hotel Royal complex. In common with the long-distance GTA, the signed path breaks off NE at first, and soon crosses a footbridge over the stream cascading out of the base of Vallone di Lourousa. In the cover of woodland, an old game track begins its seemingly never-ending zigzag climb SE. ▶

Evidence of former grazing activity comes in the form of the first of a series of abandoned huts, Gias Lagarot (1917m). From there it's not far to a noteworthy boulder,

Deciduous trees abound, their green foliage varied every now and again by the yellow blossom of laburnum. Scented green alder bushes crowd the stream, and larch take over as height is gained.

177

Terme di Valdieri

plastered with plaques in memory of perished mountaineers. At the halfway mark, the lovely grassy basin **Lagarot di Lourousa** (1970m) affords a superb view up to notorious Canalone di Lourousa. This vertiginous 45° gully, rising 900m in height and occupied by a tongue of ice, has claimed the life of many a climber on the Argentera. Incredibly this was the route taken by Coolidge and the Almers on their pioneering 1879 ascent of the massif. On the other hand Corno Stella, the 3050m trapezoidal mountain located where the gully changes direction, was first scaled in 1903 by Count Victor De Cessole. Its neighbour is the jagged Catene delle Guide. ▸

The tiny red dot of landmark Bivacco Varrone can just be made out in the *canalone* well below the crest.

Continue inexorably upwards past the last weather-beaten trees to the bare stony environs of the hut. However, unless it's your final destination (**Rifugio Morelli-Buzzi** 2351m, 3hr 15min) it's worth giving it a miss for the moment and plodding on for the pass.

Heading SSE, approaching the increasingly sheer flanks of Monte Stella, you proceed across steep rocky terrain where snow lies late into summer on this northern approach. At **Colle del Chiapous** (2526m, 40min) – the name is derived from 'slabs of rock' – vast horizons open up to reveal the craggy grey Fenestrelle ridges and twin-peaked Gelàs, with its remnant snowfield in the distance SSE. Below is the Chiotas lake and Rifugio Genova, hidden from sight by a false col in front of the pass.

Return to **Rifugio Morelli-Buzzi** (2351m, 30min), for rest and restoration if needed, before retracing your steps all the knee-trying way back down Vallone di Lourousa. From this angle the sheer mass of Monte Matto can be admired dominating the Terme. Further down the rooftops of the hotel complex come into sight through the tree branches, and in no time you're on the valley floor back at the **Terme di Valdieri** (1368m, 2hr 15min).

Rifugio Morelli-Buzzi ☎ (39) 0171 973940 CAI sleeps 45, open 15 June to 30 September, hot shower.

WALK 18

Traversing Colle di Fenestrelle

Walking Time	5hr or 1 day
Difficulty	Grade 2
Distance	16.2km/10 miles
Ascent/Descent	928m/1250m
Start/Finish	Lago della Rovina/San Giacomo
Access	From Entracque a narrow road climbs past the Piastra dam then forks: the R branch goes up Valle della Rovina, terminating at Lago della Rovina (10km from Entracque); the L branch proceeds to San Giacomo (9km from Entracque), the walk's end. A summer shuttle bus serves both.

This is a fascinating and varied walk, dominated at the start by large-scale hydroelectric projects dating back to the 1970s. Valle della Rovina, where the walk begins, is home to two dammed lakes: flow from upper Lago del Chiotas (also called Bacino artificiale del Chiotas) feeds the pumping station below Lago della Piastra on the outskirts of Entracque, where the Electricity Board (ENEL) runs a visitor centre. The most powerful hydroelectric plant in Italy began operations in 1982, crucial for the activity of the industrial city of Torino.

On the other hand, Lago della Rovina is unusual for the Maritimes, as it owes its formation to an ancient landslide that obstructed the valley with a natural barrier, behind which meltwater from ice and snow fields accumulated. DW Freshfield described it like this after a visit in 1880: 'The Lago della Rovina is a charming mountain tarn, perhaps two-thirds of a mile long. Its transparent waters are hemmed in by wooded cliffs, and the valley beyond is closed by a high barrier. The bottom is very deep and singularly smooth, except where a mass of boulders has fallen into it.'

The walk climbs past the top dam and lake, a superb viewing point for the Argentera, at 3297m the highest

Walk 18: Traversing
Colle di Fenestrelle

to Entracque

to Entracque

Valle della Rovina

PARCO NATURALE DELLE
ALPI MARITTIME

Lago della Rovina

P

**SAN
GIACOMO**
1213m

Ⓢ

P

Lago Chiotas
1978m

Rocce di Laura ▲

Punta
▲ *Ciamberline*
2792m

*Vallone di
Fenestrelle*

2010m
fork

**Rifugio
Genova**
2015m

*Colle di
Fenestrelle*
2463m

**Punta delle
Lobbie**
2322m
▲

Vallone del Cesso della Barra

N

0   1
▬▬▬▬▬▬▬ km

1800m
junction

**Rifugio
Soria Ellena**
1840m

The Chiotas dam wall and the Argentera

massif in the whole of the Maritime Alps. It continues to a panoramic col before launching on a long but enjoyable descent to Vallon del Gesso della Barra, overshadowed by Monte Gelàs. The conclusion is at the historic hamlet of San Giacomo. En route short detours lead to two convenient refuges, should you be in need of refreshment, or are contemplating an overnight stay.

WALK

From the car park at **Lago della Rovina** (1535m) at the foot of the soaring Chiotas dam wall head S past the snack bar. A key decision is imminent, as two routes present themselves. The signed path due S is shorter but quite steep and not always in good condition, due to the 'ruinous' (*rovina*) state of the rock. The more leisurely option is the longer wider track that swings NNE then SSW, but be aware that it too is subject to rock slides, and consequently is inadvisable in bad weather and stormy conditions. ◄

Ibex are common on both routes, as is the ancient king saxifrage, but only to eyes keenly scanning rock surfaces overhead for its trademark rosettes.

182

The two routes join at 1900m beneath the Rocce di Laura and proceed past a concrete chute and up to the edge of **Lago Chiotas** (also called Bacino artificiale del Chiotas) (1980m, 1hr 30min). The dam wall here measures 130m in height and 230m in length. When it was flooded in the 1970s, in the interests of hydroelectricity, a historic building was submerged – the Maritimes' very first rifugio, dating back to 1898. In compensation the Electricity Commission donated a comfortable modern structure, Rifugio Genova (see below), which stands nearby. However, visitors will undoubtedly be more interested in the amazing sight that greets them – the west face of the breathtaking Argentera rearing up over the water.

Turn L (SE) along the dirt road. At the signed **2010m fork** (15min) branch L uphill, unless Rifugio Genova calls.

Detour to Rifugio Genova (15min)
Stick to the lakeside track to Rifugio Genova (2015m, 15min).

In common with the GTA long-distance route, the clear path makes its way E amidst shrubs and wildflowers. This problem-free ascent of Vallone di Fenestrelle gives you plenty of opportunity to admire the improving vistas of the Argentera, lakes and passes below. Innumerable hairpin bends lead upward in a vast semicircle beneath the imposing barrier of Rocce di Laura. A final stretch S leads across rainbow-coloured rock and past the twin tarns that precede **Colle di Fenestrelle** (2463m, 1hr 30min), where snow patches often persist well into summer. ▶

A large colony of ibex lives here over the summer months, perching on the crags either side that rise to the Punta and Roc di Fenestrelle.

With exciting views to the elongated summit ridge of Gelàs SE, the descent path proceeds SSE in graded zigzags beneath Punta delle Lobbie, crossing vast grassy slopes where chamois graze. After the ruins of a herder's hut at Gias Alvé, a sizeable boulder marking a **1800m junction** (1hr 30min) in Piano del Praiet is reached.

183

> **Detour to Rifugio Soria Ellena (10min)**
> Cut up the opposite slope past an old shepherds' hut to hospitable Rifugio Soria Ellena (1840m), beautifully placed beneath the giant Gelàs. See Walk 9 for more details.

The gushing torrent of meltwater from elevated ice and snow fields is a constant companion with its delightful sound, while green alder bushes dot the surrounding slopes.

Turn L (NNE) on the rough jeep track that makes its bumpy way down Vallone del Gesso della Barra; walkers can take the occasional short-cut. To the SSE the Gelàs massif and Ray della Siula can be admired at length. ◄

The road improves a little at a clearing and sign in memory of wartime refugees who fled this way (see Walk 6 for more on this). The surrounding mountainsides gradually turn fresh green with dense beech woods. A short distance downhill is the hamlet of **San Giacomo** (1213m, 1hr 45min).

Accommodation is available at the Park Foresteria and the camping ground. There's also a park visitor centre and café-restaurant.

Rifugio Genova ☎ (39) 0171 978138 CAI, sleeps 60, open 15 June to 15 September, hot shower, credit cards www.rifugiogenova.it.

Rifugio Soria Ellena ☎ (39) 0171 978382 CAI, sleeps 62, open 15 June to 15 September, hot shower www.rifugiosoriaellena.com. (See Walk 9 for more details.)

San Giacomo
Park Foresteria ☎ (39) 0171 978444, sleeps 20, open mid-June to mid-September, hot shower, cooking facilities

Sotto il Faggio camp ground ☎ mobile (39) 349 7305438, open June to September

WALK 19
Rifugio Pagari Loop

Walking Time	9hr 20min or 2 days
Difficulty	Grade 2+
Distance	21.5km/13.3 miles
Ascent/Descent	1537m/1537m
Start/Finish	San Giacomo
Access	From Entracque a narrow 9km road follows Vallone del Gesso della Barra, terminating at San Giacomo, where parking is available. A summer shuttle bus covers the same route.

Opening with a stiff climb of 1437m, this stunning loop route explores the elevated realms of 'hidden valley' Vallone del Muraion, overshadowed by imposing 3000m-plus giants Gelàs and Cima della Maledia. The latter comes from 'cursed', as once upon a time all mountains, inaccessible places of rock and snow, were considered atrocious and damnable.

Dotted with picturesque lakes, snow fields and small glaciers, it is a stark landscape, yet both wildflowers and animals come in large concentrations. Panoramas aren't exactly in short supply either, especially during the traverse in Stage 2. At a stretch, very fit walkers can complete the walk in a single day, though it's a pity to miss a stopover at Rifugio Pagari, the highest manned hut in the whole of the Maritime Alps. On the other hand, with the appropriate gear (sleeping bag, cooking equipment and food) by all means stay overnight at well-placed Bivacco Moncalieri, a short way above the lake in Stage 2.

The curiously name Pagari comes from Paganino dal Pozzo, a visionary 15th-century constructor of mule tracks-cum-trade routes across the Maritime Alps. Commissioned by the influential Savoia family to find a shorter route, he built one across 2819m Passo Pagari, later named in his honour (not far from the refuge).

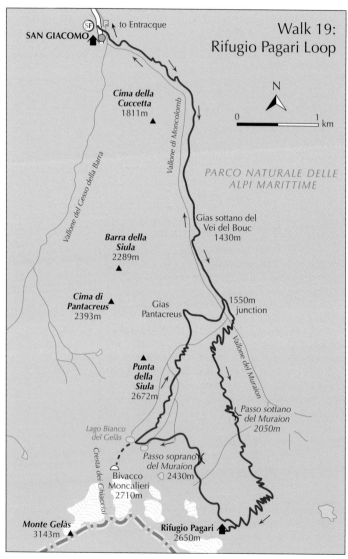

San Giacomo

SF

P

to Entracque

Walk 19:
Rifugio Pagari Loop

*Cima della
Cuccetta*
1811m ▲

N

0   1
km

Vallone di Moncolomb

*PARCO NATURALE DELLE
ALPI MARITTIME*

Vallone del Cesso della Barra

Gias sottano del
Vei del Bouc
1430m

*Barra della
Siula*
2289m
▲

*Cima di
Pantacreus*
2393m ▲

Gias
Pantacreus

1550m
junction

Vallone del Muraion

▲
*Punta
della
Siula*
2672m

*Lago Bianco
del Gelàs*

*Passo sottano
del Muraion*
2050m

Cresta dei Ghiacciai

Bivacco
Moncalieri
2710m

*Passo soprano
del Muraion*
2430m

Monte Gelàs
3143m ▲

Rifugio Pagari
2650m

Sunset from Rifugio Pagari

However, over time the unstable terrain, lack of pasture for the mules and glacial expansion led to its closure – and Pagari's financial ruin.

At the walk start the cluster of buildings that makes up San Giacomo includes comfortable walkers accommodation in place of its long-gone pilgrims hospice: Foresteria (☎ (39) 0171 978444, sleeps 20, open mid-June to mid-September, hot shower, cooking facilities) or the camping ground Sotto il Faggio (☎ mobile (39) 349 7305438, open June to September). There's also a park visitor centre and café-restaurant.

STAGE 1
San Giacomo to Rifugio Pagari

Walking Time	4hr 50min
Difficulty	Grade 2
Distance	11.3km/7 miles
Ascent	1437m

Old moraine ridges en route to Rifugio Pagari

After a stroll along a pasture valley, the path wastes no time in gaining height, entering a high-altitude realm of vast rockscapes and wildlife.

From the car park near the camping ground at **San Giacomo** (1213m) on the eastern bank of Torrente Gesso della Barra, turn SE into Vallone di Moncolomb (the name derives from 'far pass or place', a reference to high distant pastures). The rough track climbs through stunning ancient beech woods, passing a former *casa reale di caccia,* where the royal family and their entourage would stay during hunting forays. It now operates as a family summer retreat. Delicious spring water is on tap at the rear of the building.

After a narrowish passage where the valley is squeezed by Cima della Cuccetta, all of a sudden the pasture Pra del Rasur opens up, and you continue due S in the company of grazing cows, chamois and old *gias* (shepherds' huts). Ahead is the tantalising sight of snow-spattered Mont Clapier, Cima di Pagari and Maledia, towering over glacier pockets.

At **Gias sottano del Vei del Bouc** (1430m, 1hr 15min) keep R (Walk 20 forks L here). The main stream is soon crossed on a log bridge, and a further 20min on is the 1550m branch for Lago Bianco del Gelàs, where the route returns in Stage 2. Ignore it this time round.

Soon afterwards you may get wet boots crossing Rio Pantacreus, though planks are usually in place. Keep mostly S alongside cascades shaded by rowan and laburnum trees with green alder, while on ground level are bilberry plants and luxuriant ferns, not to mention darting lizards. An especially well-preserved stretch of mule track SSE reaches the superb lookout of **Passo sottano del Muraion** (2050m, 1hr) opposite the jagged crest of Cima del Tor (E).

You are now well and truly in the beautiful realms of Vallone del Muraion, a magnificent glacial amphitheatre with ridges of ancient moraine and glimpses of ice from shrinking glaciers. As the last Arolla pines peter out, carpets of pink alpenrose take over. An old hut invaded by nettles is passed, affording great views to the perfect funnel moraine below Mont Clapier. An abrupt veer SW requires a final effort on wide curves up into a striking world of rock and snow. The hut flag comes into sight at the very last moment, as does a miniature botanical garden at

3hr 35min – Rifugio Pagari (also called Rifugio Federici-Marchesini) (2650m). ☎ (39) 0171 978398, CAI, sleeps 24, open 15 June to 15 September www.rifugiopagari. com. A veritable eyrie, run lovingly by an aesthete who prepares delicious vegetarian meals (along with home-brewed beer), it offers little in the way of mod cons – a trifling drawback abundantly compensated for by the magical setting. The hut is a key base for mountaineers exploring the surrounding peaks. Views range from Cima del Lago dell'Agnel NE and even distant Monviso NW. Take a wander at the rear of the hut, in the company of ibex, towards the surviving glaciers sheltering on the northern flanks of the ridge linking Cima di Pagari with Maledia.

Inquisitive young ibex near Bivacco Moncalieri

STAGE 2
Rifugio Pagari to San Giacomo

Walking Time	4hr 30min
Difficulty	Grade 2
Distance	10.2km/6.3 miles
Ascent/Descent	100m/1537m

Here a beautiful but marginally exposed path cuts across dizzy mountainsides below Cima della Maledia to a lovely lake. Next comes an enjoyable if particularly steep descent via cascading streams before the outward route is resumed in Vallon di Moncolomb and back to San Giacomo.

From **Rifugio Pagari** (2650m) go back down to the fork L (signed for Bivacco Moncalieri) and drop across the hut's water pipe. A clear path leads NNW, initially skirting below Caire del Muraion. It loses a little height to **Passo soprano del Muraion** (2430m) and its rock spur. The traces of the former hunting track end here and the way is narrower now. A short precarious passage around a crumbled flank is soon behind you, and the path reaches grassy terrain thick with lilac-flowered adenostyle. It proceeds in gradual ascent WNW to a stream crossing smooth rocks, soon veering L up over rubble past a first 2501m lake, to

1hr 30min – Lago Bianco del Gelàs (2553m) at the foot of Punta della Siula.

Extension to Bivacco Moncalieri (1hr return)

Time permitting, it's well worth continuing SSW on the clear path with the ibex to Bivacco Moncalieri (2710m, 30min) below Cresta dei Ghiacciai (crossed in Walk 12). The fantastic views NW extend to triangular Monviso and the spread of the Cuneo plain. The sturdy timber and metal hut sleeps nine, and water can be found nearby. It replaces an older, lower structure on the lakeside, swept away by an avalanche in 1975.

At the three-way arrows painted on a rock at the lake's edge, turn N for the descent route via Vallone di Pantacreus. A series of rock terraces and grassy banks of alpenrose are negotiated on paths that get very steep in places. Follow the red paint stripes carefully. You drop alongside a lovely waterfall and descend precipitously over grassy terrain to cross to the L bank of Rio Pantacreus. More zigzagging steepness follows, over stony ground, before a relatively restful stretch NNW with a few ups and downs.

At **Gias Pantacreus** (1862m) the path veers ESE to head through a beech copse. Overgrown sections ensue, then it's along a mini-gorge with the cascading stream. You finally reach the **1550m junction** (1hr 40min) where you pick up the Rifugio Pagari access path. Turn L downhill, retracing your steps from Stage 1 via **Gias sottano del Vei del Bouc** (1430m), to the walk conclusion at **3hr – San Giacomo (1213m).**

Delicious drinking water at San Giacomo

WALK 20
Vallon del Vei del Bouc

Walking Time	4hr 45min or 1 day
Difficulty	Grade 1–2
Distance	15km/9.3miles
Ascent/Descent	841m/841m
Start/Finish	San Giacomo
Access	See Walk 19

The curious name Vei del Bouc, applied to valley, lake and pass alike, was long believed to mean *il vecchio del caprone*, 'the old goat man', a legendary figure who eked out a solitary existence in a high cirque. As the story goes, when he died the stream swelled to the dimensions of a lake to protect his last resting place, covering all traces. In a decidedly less romantic vein, scholars claim the expression derives from a distorted version of 'walled enclosure for livestock', pointing to the presence of herders. To boost this hypothesis, there are faded prehistoric rock inscriptions near the water's edge. Dating back 4000 years, they closely resemble those around Mont Bégo over the border in France, and may well be linked to seasonal livestock movements in ancient times.

The walk itself follows easy paths in the footsteps of the king's hunting parties. A recommended extension is given – to a nearby walkers' peak (Grade 2), alias stunning lookout – allow an extra 2hr 20min.

WALK
At **San Giacomo** (1213m) follow the road and cross to the eastern bank of Torrente Gesso della Barra, turning R (SE) for Vallone di Moncolomb. The track climbs through stunning ancient beech woods, passing a former *casa reale di caccia*, where royal entourages used to stay during hunting forays. It is now a family summer retreat. Delicious spring water is available at the rear of the building.

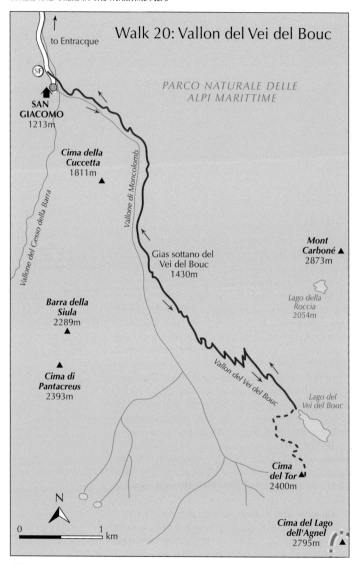

Walk 20: Vallon del Vei del Bouc

to Entracque

SF

SAN GIACOMO
1213m

Cima della Cuccetta
1811m ▲

PARCO NATURALE DELLE ALPI MARITTIME

Vallone di Moncolomb

Vallone del Cesso della Barra

Gias sottano del Vei del Bouc
1430m

Mont Carboné ▲
2873m

Lago della Roccia
2054m

Barra della Siula
2289m ▲

Cima di Pantacreus
2393m ▲

Vallon del Vei del Bouc

Lago del Vei del Bouc

Cima del Tor ▲
2400m

N

0   1 km

Cima del Lago dell'Agnel
2795m ▲

After a narrowish passage where the valley is squeezed by Cima della Cuccetta, pasture-flat Pra del Rasur unexpectedly opens up. Now you continue due S, in the company of grazing cows, chamois and old *gias* shepherds' huts. Ahead snow-spattered peaks crown the valley.

Lago del Vei del Bouc

At key junction **Gias sottano del Vei del Bouc** (1hr 15min, 1430m) branch L (see Walk 19 for Rifugio Pagari, which forks R here). Above the treeline this is a steady, problem-free climb SE on what's left of an old hunting track, its wide curves almost restful. These grassy slopes can be hot and dry in summer, with large numbers of crickets, while flowers are similarly abundant, with milfoil, pinks and showy thistles. Views across S to Cima Pagari and its neighbours improve with every step you take.

Up at the 2000m mark, be sure to branch R across the lake's outlet and up over a lip to **Lago del Vei del Bouc** (2054m, 1hr 30min). Masses of roches mountonnées, reminiscent of recumbent whales and even dinosaur

An old hunting track climbs high to Cima del Tor

shapes, are everywhere, witnesses to the long-gone glaciers that modelled this cirque. The inviting green-hued lake is home to silvery weed and jumping trout, while on the shores herds of cows graze peacefully in the company of chamois. High above SSE is Cima del Lago dell'Agnel, on the long forbidding ridge between Italy and France. Due N is Mont Carboné, while Colle del Vei del Bouc is ESE.

Time, weather and knees permitting, it is well worth exploring a little-frequented path to Cima del Tor.

Extension to Cima del Tor (2hr 20min return)

In the proximity of the park hut near the water's edge, vestiges of an old hunting track (dotted on the commercial map) swing essentially S. Through banks of alpenrose it climbs the crest that culminates with Cima del Tor. There are astounding views as the path alternates from the outer to inner side of the shoulder. The odd collapsed tract needs scrambling over, but this is nothing of consequence. Bird's-eye views over the lake are enjoyed, and the vistas take in the Malinvern and Pagari peaks, and soon also the Argentera. At 2420m (1hr 20min) the track ends abruptly (though a faint path does continue a further 10min to an old hunting shelter standing out on a higher spur). Backtrack briefly and detour to the summit and cross on 2400m Cima del Tor.

Afterwards, 1hr will see you back down at the lakeside.

From **Lago del Vei del Bouc** (2054m) allow 2hr to return the same way to **San Giacomo** (1213m).

See Walk 19 for accommodation and facilities at San Giacomo.

WALK 21
Gorge della Reina

Walking Time	3hr or 1 day
Difficulty	Grade 1–2
Distance	7.3km/4.5 miles
Ascent/Descent	500m/500m
Start/Finish	Piazza Giustizia e Libertà, Entracque
Access	A short detour off main Valle Gesso, Entracque has year-round buses from Cuneo, and is also served by the park's summertime shuttle bus. The central square, alias the walk start, with the park info/tourist office is easily located.

A rarity for the Maritime Alps – a limestone chasm is the highlight of this fascinating, rewarding circuit. Gorge della Reina supposedly took its name from Queen Giovanna d'Angiò (also known as 'Reino Jano'), a much-loved sovereign who lived in the 14th century. She is attributed with uniting all the Occitan peoples under one flag. As the story goes, so besotted with her was the son of the king of France that when she refused his advances he called in the army (!). The queen took refuge at Roaschia (in a valley parallel to Entracque), but her unsolicited suitor dispatched his soldiers to the mountaintop for a surprise attack. However, as is the way of legends, providence stepped in, sending the entire army plummeting to their deaths in the depths of the gorge! Just goes to show...

This straightforward walk is not suitable in the mid-summer heat of the day. Even before the cool chasm, the interest level is high, thanks to constantly changing vegetation and surprisingly vast views across the Maritimes. The rock here is mostly sedimentary, and the resulting plant life remarkably rich: there's even an endemic, the bright reddish-purple *Primula allioni* (Allioni's primrose), which blooms in limestone crannies in the gorge itself. Laid-back Entracque, with its wealth of medieval

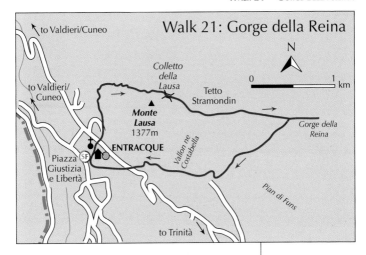

Walk 21: Gorge della Reina

fountains, also has plenty of visitor amenities, such as a bakery, well-stocked grocery shops and restaurants. There is accommodation at a camping ground or hotels.

WALK

From the picturesque square in **Entracque** (904m), Piazza Giustizia e Libertà, take Via Angelo Barale through the shopping district to Piazzale Europa. Turn R in front of the Bealetto, an 18th-century chapel where *ex votos* are left in recognition of divine assistance. Next take Via Caduti in Guerra, which has a signpost for the walk. Following red waymarks, keep R past house number 8 to a marked fork, where it's R to ascend the pleasant curves of a well-graded path across flowered meadows. The occasional views range back down to Entracque, as well as the sheer limestone flanks of Monte Lausa alongside E. Mixed woodland and deafening birdsong is followed by a cooler conifer plantation, soft needles underfoot.

At the saddle **Colletto della Lausa** (1295m, 1hr 10min) a completely different landscape awaits, with a descent of Vallon di Costabella on an earth path to the 'rear' of Monte Lausa. Open slopes are dotted with dog roses, orchids and

Gorge della Reina

birch trees. Above (N) is Monte Corno, while ahead due S is the string of peaks topped by Monte Carboné. A gentle climb passes through hazelnut thickets to a junction where you take the L fork. It's not far up to the stone houses of abandoned hamlet **Tetto Stramondin** (1225m, 20min).

Heading E under a power line, the path traverses below the sheer pink face of Rocca di Reina, the adjoining rugged limestone crests cloaked in dense wood. The concentration and variety of wildflowers is breathtaking (mountain lavender!), as are the views, which even extend to the snow-spattered Argentera.

Downhill is the entrance to the **Gorge della Reina** (1141m, 20min), but just before the valley bottom, fork L on the narrow but clear path that penetrates the canyon. Dizzy cliffs with curious horizontal strata crowd in, and saxifrage droops from nooks and crannies. Unless there has been heavy rain, the stream will be a mere trickle. By all means continue to where the chasm forks into two, the R branch ending at the base of a modest waterfall. Afterwards return to the entrance and sunlight (1141m, 30min).

Turn SW, following the L bank of the stream through beech woods, and ignore the turn-off (for Pian di Funs and its via ferrata). At a lane go L; not far along is a junction (with a via ferrata information board): branch R here across a bridge where a characterful old mule track W takes over. A short climb is followed by gentle shady descent along old terraces sustained by drystone walls. It eventually finishes at Bar L'Ariunda on Corso Francia. Cross straight over the road for Via S Antonio. Four old fountains and several changes of street name later, not to mention rows of traditional houses with arched courtyard entrances, you're back at Piazza Giustizia e Libertà in **Entracque** (904m, 40min).

Campeggio Valle Gesso ☎ (39) 0171 978247
www.campingvallegesso.com
Trois Etoiles ☎ (39) 0171 978283 www.hoteltroisetoiles.com
Miramonti ☎ (39) 0171 978222 www.hotelmiramontientracque.com

WALK 22

Vallone degli Alberghi

Walking Time	5hr or 1 day
Difficulty	Grade 2
Distance	10.5km/6.5 miles
Ascent/Descent	678m/678m
Start/Finish	Palanfré
Access	From Vernante and its railway station in Valle Vermenagna, a minor road climbs 9km to Palanfré.

Peaceful Vallone degli Alberghi is explored on this route. Penetrating the NE corner of the Maritimes, this V-profile valley culminates with a group of photogenic tarns overlooked by formidable Monte Frisson, dubbed the 'little Matterhorn' because of its elegant pyramidal shape. Geological interest is prominent, because of the meeting of sedimentary and igneous rock, which results in colourful contact lines. The central section is mostly limestone, worn into deep grooves and chasms that swallow up surface water.

A host of curious place names are encountered en route. For a start, due to a transcription error from 'arbergh', Vallone degli Alberghi, rather than meaning 'valley of the hotels', means 'last pasture', refering to pastoral activity practised here for centuries, and ongoing today. Palanfré has been traced back to a late medieval term for 'cart horses', though more plausible is 'isolated place at the foot of steep grassy slopes and cliffs', an apt description. Mighty Monte Frisson at the valley head owes its derivation to an ancient French term for 'shiver', in view of the freezing winds that blow across here. Not surprisingly, its neighbour Monte Ciamoussè's name means 'rugged terrain frequented by chamois'.

The walk start is pretty Palanfré, set on the edge of beautiful beech woods that turn pure gold in autumn. The hamlet has an excellent dairy and a lovely restaurant

Walk 22: Vallone degli Alberghi

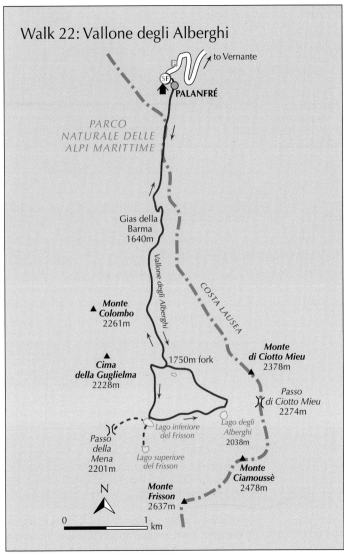

to Vernante

PALANFRÉ

*PARCO
NATURALE DELLE
ALPI MARITTIME*

Gias della
Barma
1640m

Vallone degli Alberghi

COSTA LAUSEA

▲ *Monte
Colombo*
2261m

▲
*Cima
della Guglielma*
2228m

1750m fork

*Monte
di Ciotto Mieu*
2378m

*Passo
di Ciotto Mieu*
2274m

*Lago inferiore
del Frisson*

*Lago degli
Alberghi*
2038m

)(
*Passo
della
Mena*
2201m

*Lago superiore
del Frisson*

▲ *Monte
Ciamoussè*
2478m

N

*Monte
Frisson*
2637m

0   1
km

Lago inferiore del Frisson and Monte Frisson

and guesthouse, owned by the park authority, that serves local products. Otherwise stay at Vernante; the Relais del Nazionale will drive its guests to the walk start.

Note The route climbs to beautiful Lago inferiore del Frisson, where two short extensions are described. It then takes a high link path across to Lago degli Alberghi, although at the time of writing it was not in the best condition, due to rock falls, so be prepared to turn back if needs be and retrace your steps. If all goes well, after the second lake, the return stretch takes a look at the other fork of Vallone degli Alberghi, before returning to Palanfré.

An additional walk suggestion: highly panoramic Costa di Planard and Colle della Garbella are visited on Walk 23, and can also be reached from Palanfré – 950m height gain in 2hr 30min.

WALK

From the car park at **Palanfré** (1379m) head uphill through the hamlet and past a fountain spouting deliciously cool water, continuing past the dairy. A lane branches R at the first bend, but you proceed straight ahead (S) on a broad path through beech woods following the park border. After a leisurely level stroll the trees are left behind. Past another gushing fountain and tiny huts, you keep to the R side of the narrowing valley for a steep winding climb. In the stream below swirling stones have excavated a series of kettles – bowl-shaped depressions known as le buriere, for their resemblance to butter churns. Opposite are the curious grooved limestone slabs of Costa Lausea, embedded with tiny lens-shaped nummulite fossils.

The gradient eases as you enter a shady corridor. Huge boulders are passed, and the streambed is full of bleached boulders, but little water, as it has has momentarily sunk underground, reappearing further up as an icy cold flow. The valley narrows a little as the path climbs gently at the foot of Monte Colombo, its steep slopes colonised by scented dwarf mountain pine.

At a signed **1750m fork** (1hr 30min), where the loop returns later, turn R. This climbs steadily to reach a platform and summer farm **Gias Vilazzo** (1823m), backed by Monte Ciamoussè SE and Monte Frisson SSE. In the

At Lago inferiore del Frisson

opposite direction the Piemonte plain opens out, with the city of Cuneo visible.

Further uphill the path soon overlooks diminutive Lago Villazzo, the result of a rock fall. A rounded ancient rock barrier is climbed, amid spreads of alpenrose, and at the very last minute you reach the beautiful shores of **Lago inferiore del Frisson** (2057m, 50min), the lower of the twin lakes. They have been dubbed the 'mirrors' of the Frisson, as both reflect the slender peak.

Detours to Lago superiore del Frisson and Passo della Mena

After a well-earned picnic, consider following the water's edge R for the clear path up to 2127m Lago superiore del Frisson (allow 30min return). Alternatively, follow signs up the narrowing and slightly exposed path to 2201m Passo della Mena (50min return) for great views into the rugged heart of the Italian Maritime Alps.

Now branch E for the narrow path that makes its way over an uneven ridge that descends directly from Monte Frisson. Rough, undulating terrain is traversed, and the way is not always clear, so keep your eyes peeled for red waymarks. Your goal is the deep glacial cirque with another pretty tarn, **Lago degli Alberghi** (2038m, 40min), at the foot of Monte Ciamoussè.

Now it's L as the GTA route is joined below Passo di Ciotto Mieu, to head NW across terraced pastures popular with cows and chamois. The gradient steepens as you descend to the refreshing torrent, where tired sweaty feet can be cooled off. It's not far from the 1750m fork.

Take the same path followed earlier on in leisurely descent to return to **Palanfré** (1379m, 2hr).

L'Albergh del Parco ☎ (39) 334 3052503, sleeps 30, hot shower, always open (phone to check early and late season), dorms for walkers

WALK 23
Costa di Planard

Walking Time	4hr 30min or 1 day
Difficulty	Grade 2
Distance	9.5km/5.9 miles
Ascent/Descent	1079m/1079m
Start/Finish	Trinità
Access	See Walk 21 for Entracque, then follow Corso Francia out of town for the 5km drive to Trinità.

The eastern sector of the Maritimes lacks convenient access and staging structures such as manned huts. Though once key arteries for trade routes, such as the *vie del sale* (salt routes), these days the deep valleys see few two-legged visitors, so nature is left to run its course. This walk climbs to a vantage point par excellence high over the wild Bousset and Sabbione valleys. The destination is elongated Costa di Planard (sometimes spelt Pianard) for brilliant views into the jagged heart of the Maritimes and further afield. It's a fair slog, demanding a height gain in excess of 1000m (just). Paths are clear and straightforward, though a little exposed close to the crest.

Bird lovers will especially enjoy late summer here, as Costa di Planard is on a major migration route, and considerable numbers of birds of prey transit, also attracted by the open grassy slopes on the eastern side.

At the walk start in Vallone del Bousset, a cluster of old farmhouses and a little church go by the name of Trinità. In 1939 Queen Elena had a primary school built there. It taught the three Rs until inhabitants dwindled away to the mere handful left in summer nowadays. The building has been tastefully converted by the park authority into a restaurant, walkers' hostel and guest house.

Walk 23: Costa di Planard

PARCO NATURALE DELLE ALPI MARITTIME

to Entracque

Tetti Prer
1155m

TRINITÀ

Vallone Grande

Caire di
Porcera
1818m

Monte
Pianard ▲
2306m

Vallone del Bousset

Ponte di Porcera
1088m

Colle della
Garbella
2170m

Costa di Planard

Vallone del Bousset

N

0   1
         km

WALK

From Locanda del Sorriso at **Trinità** (1091m) follow the road a short way uphill E, and where the tarmac curves L (for Tetti Prer) fork R onto a lane. In common with the red/white waymarks of the GTA, this ventures into Vallone Grande and woodland. Around the 1300m mark a path takes over and approaches an inviting stream and pool at the opening of a dramatic gorge.

However, this is quickly left behind as a steep ascent SE ensues (slippery if wet). Slopes cloaked with beech, and harbouring flowers such as rosebay willowherb and exquisite martagon lilies, are crossed. Zigzags SE climb to a scenic saddle close to tower-like Caire di Porcera. Cutting the westernmost flanks of Monte Planard and alternating steep sections with a softer gradient, a narrow path embarks on a lengthy diagonal traverse high over Vallone del Bousset.

Colle della Garbella (2170m, 2hr 30min) is finally reached. The reward is exceptional views – as far as the triangle of Monviso, which stands out NW, and into the very heart of the Maritimes, with its multitudinous orange-brown teeth-like tips. The Argentera is discernible W beyond the Carboné-Aiera line-up, while in the opposite direction is the Bisalta.

Consider wandering towards Monte Garbella further S along the grassy ridge, thick with ground-hugging juniper and alpenrose, to drink in this marvellous atmosphere, or even embark on the optional ascent of 2306m Monte Planard NNW.

Return the same way. This direction gives you plenty of opportunity to admire the elegant limestone terraces of Costa di Raiet that dominate the horizon over Entracque. Watch your step on the steep sections as you go back to the peaceful hamlet of **Trinità** (1091m, 2hr).

Locanda del Sorriso ☎ (39) 0171 978388, sleeps 38, open June to September and other times on reservation, hot shower, credit cards www.locandadelsorriso.com

Colle della Garbella

WALK 24

The Border Forts

Walking Time	4hr or 1 day
Difficulty	Grade 2
Distance	14km/8.7 miles
Ascent/Descent	450m/450m
Start/Finish	Chalet Le Marmotte near Col de Tende
Access	On the SS20 in upper Valle Vermenagna above Limone, close to the entrance of the road tunnel to France, a road forks off via the ski resort Panice Soprana 1400. Mostly surfaced, its countless switchbacks climb to Col de Tende. Access is also possible from the French side, but only for 4WDs. A year-round bus from Limone and the railway station runs as far as the ski resort.

The concluding walk in this guidebook to the Maritime Alps of France and Italy explores the grassy crest and watershed separating the two countries. Nowadays the peaceful surroundings of Col de Tende (also called Colle di Tenda) are enjoyed by the odd walker and cyclist, but it has been used as a route assiduously since ancient times, and is rich in history, as it was one of the easiest passages between the Piemonte plain and the Mediterranean coast. Of their visit during a 1861 grand tour, the adventurous Catlow sisters wrote: '... the ascent is rapid, but by a very good but steep alpine road, some turns of which are a little alarming from their abruptness and want of defence, but soon giving to view the most beautiful forms of the Maritime Alps, with Monte Viso as the crowning charm. The view from the summit is magnificent, and amply repays any little tremors caused by the ascent...'

A final historical note is *de rigeur*. Back in 1882 Italy joined the Triple Alliance with the Austro-Hungarian Empire and Germany, which transformed neighbouring France into a potential enemy. A large-scale outlay of funds went into the construction of military roads through

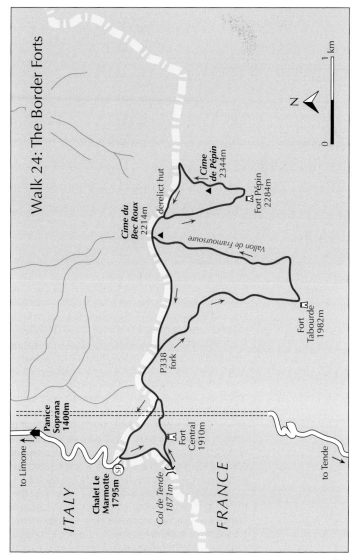

Walk 24: The Border Forts

Cime de Pépin
2344m

derelict hut

Cime du Bec Roux
2214m

Fort Pépin
2284m

Vallon de Framousoure

Fort Tabourde
1982m

P338
fork

Panice Soprana 1400m

to Limone

Chalet Le Marmotte 1795m

SF

Fort Central 1910m

Col de Tende 1871m

FRANCE

ITALY

to Tende

0   1 km

N

Magnificent Rocca dell'Abisso from Col de Tende

the strategic mountainous border areas, punctuated with huge forts. Three are visited on this walk. (The other three forts – Pernante, Giaure and Marguerie – are west of the pass.) In wonderfully panoramic spots, they are extraordinary examples of architecture, albeit for the purposes of war. Each is surrounded by a moat and accessible by drawbridge.

Despite much crisscrossing of the border, the walk is in France for the most part and is best followed on the IGN 1:25,000 map, sheet 3841 OT (Vallée de la Roya). The terrain is mainly grassy with breathtaking concentrations of wildflowers that colour entire mountainsides, with the added bonus of eagles and other birds of prey hunting in the open. Clear weather conditions are best for taking in the vast views – and finding the way, as landmarks are few and far between.

Chalet Le Marmotte, where the walk starts and ends, has refreshments and good meals though no accommodation. The most convenient hotel is Tres Amis at Panice Soprana 1400; the friendly owner will drive guests up to the pass.

WALK

From **Chalet Le Marmotte** (1795m) and its flagpoles walk S up the short stretch of rough road to **Col de Tende** (1871m, 10min) and the Italo–French border. On the horizon WNW is the triangle of Monte Frisson alongside pale-grey Rocca dell'Abisso (W), which rises gracefully; its descriptive name 'abyss' is linked to its dizzy northern face, though curiously the Provencal root *bis* means 'freezing wind'. It was described as 'a trifling hump' by WM Conway in 1894!

Turn L along the lane past the extensive old barracks to the sprawl of **Fort Central** (1910m, 10min), the most impressive of the six forts, with lots to explore.

The lane descends to join a wider track NE (turn R), passing below rocks studded with saxifrage. At the **P338 fork** turn R past a traffic barrier to embark on a panoramic stroll SES beneath vast spreads of alpenrose. Alpine choughs wheel overhead, and skylarks have a field day here. The path finishes at the strategic promontory where ruined **Fort Tabourde** (1982m, 40min) is located. It affords amazing views of the 52 tortuous curves of the old road snaking its way down to Vallée de la Roya in France.

A clear if narrower path leads around the corner ENE through a veritable rock garden, with scores of Mediterranean plant species. Above herders' huts, you cross the shallow pasture fold of Vallon de Framoursoure, veering N uphill following a trickling stream. Despite optimistic maps, there is no trace on the ground of the path cutting diagonally SE to Fort Pépin, so continue upward through marmot territory on a rutted path to emerge on a former military track a little below the international crest a short distance NE of Cime du Bec Roux.

Turn R (E) for the zigzagging ascent – or short-cut – through a smother of edelweiss and tiny vanilla orchids. The graceful limestone massif of Marguareis NE is soon in view. Once you've reached a signed junction near a **derelict hut**, fork R for a highly panoramic amble SSE to the half-buried ruins of **Fort Pépin** (2284m, 1hr 10min) on a promontory.

Fort Central

Here yellow paint stripes lead L through the ruins to where a narrow path follows a line of wall and soon tackles an eroded gully – watch your step. It quickly returns to grassy flowered slopes NNE cutting across Cime de Pépin. At 2208m you slot L (NNW) into the clear GTA route on the principal ridge, all but smothered with pink alpenrose.

The junction near the **derelict hut** is not far off, then it's plain sailing past the foot of Cime du Bec Roux, along the Franco–Italian border, with plentiful red/white markings. The ski slopes and resort of Panice Soprana 1400 lie below. Take care not to miss the branch R for the narrow path that puts knees to the test as it negotiates an abrupt mountainside in the company of green alder and raspberries.

Back down at the **P338 fork** you can finally take it easy on the almost level track once more. Around the rocky corner ignore the detour to Fort Central and part ways with the GTA as you bear NW back to **Chalet Le Marmotte** (1795m, 1hr 50min).

Panice Soprana 1400
Hotel Tres Amis ☎ (39) 0171 928175 www.hotel3amis.it

APPENDIX 1
French–English and Italian–English Glossaries

French–English

alpe, alpage	mountain pasture
arrêt d'autobus	bus stop
au secours!	help!
baisse	mountain pass, usually broad and grassy
balisage	waymarking
barrage	dam
bas	low
bassin	basin
blockhaus	old military construction, bunker
bois	wood
cabanne	hut
câble métallique	cable (ie aided route)
cabret, cabrera	place for goats
caire	sharp rocky point
cairn	cairn, heap of stones as path marker
car	bus
carte de randonnée	walking map
cascade	waterfall
chambre/dortoir	bedroom/dormitory
chaussures de montagne	walking boots
chute de pierres	rock falls
cime	mountain summit
croix	cross
danger	danger
descente	descent
difficile/facile	difficult/easy
douche froide/chaude	cold/hot shower
droite/gauche	right/left
eau (non) potable	water (not) drinkable
étape	walk stage
fermé/ouvert	closed/open
fleuve, rivière	river, stream
forêt	forest
gare	railway station
gare routière	bus station
gîte d'étape	walkers' hostel
glace/glacier	ice/glacier
gravure	rock engraving
grotte	cave
haut, élevé	high
haute route	high-level walking route
haut plateau	high-lying plateau
horaire	timetable
jardin alpin	Alpine botanical garden
lac	lake
mauvais	bad
météo	weather forecast
montée	ascent
neige	snow
névé firn	snow field
pas	mountain pass
piste	lane, 4WD track
pont	bridge
racccourci	short-cut
rando/randonnée	walk
randonneur	walker
refuge	mountain hut, often manned
route	road
secours en montagne	mountain rescue
sentier	path
source	spring
table d'orientation	orientation table
téléphérique à matériaux	aerial cableway for goods
torrent	mountain river or stream
vacherie	summer dairy farm
vallée, vallon	valley
vire	ledge

Italian–English

acqua (non) potabile	water (not) drinkable
aiuto!	help!
alpe	mountain pasture
alta via	high-level walking route
alto, elevato	high
altopiano	high-lying plateau
aperto/chiuso	open/closed
autostazione	bus station
bacino	basin, lake
basso	low
bosco	wood
caduta sassi	rock falls
camera/dormitorio	bedroom/dormitory

215

capanna	hut	*incisione rupestre*	rock engraving
carta escursionistica	walking map	*lago*	lake
cascata	waterfall	*nevaio*	snow field
caserma	barracks	*nuovo percorso*	new routing
cattivo, brutto	bad	*ometto*	cairn, lit. 'little man'
cavo, fune metallica	cable (ie aided route)	*orario*	timetable
cengia	ledge	*passo*	mountain pass or saddle
cima	mountain summit	*pericolo*	danger
col	hill, mountain or saddle	*pian*	level ground
croce	cross	*piccolo*	small
cuccetta	bunk bed	*pista*	lane, 4WD track
destra/sinistra	right/left (direction)	*ponte*	bridge
difficile/facile	difficult/easy	*previsione del tempo*	weather forecast
diga	dam	*pronto soccorso*	first aid
discesa	descent	*rifugio*	manned mountain hut
doccia fredda/calda	cold/hot shower	*rio, torrente*	mountain stream
fermata dell'autobus	bus stop	*salita*	ascent
fiume	river	*scarponi*	walking boots
fontana	fountain	*scorciatoia*	short-cut
fonte, sorgente	spring	*sentiero*	path
foresta	forest	*soccorso alpino*	mountain rescue
foresteria, posto tappa	walkers' hostel	*stazione ferroviaria*	railway station
galleria	tunnel	*strada*	road
ghiaccio/ghiacciaio	ice/glacier	*tappa*	stage of walk
giardino alpino	Alpine botanical garden	*teleferica*	aerial cableway for goods
gias	herding place, shepherds' hut	*tetto, tetti*	hamlet
giro	tour	*val, valle*	valley
grotta	cave		

APPENDIX 2
Walk Summary Table

Walk	Time	Days	Distance	Ascent/Descent	Grade	Page
1	4hr 30min	1 day	17km/10.5 miles	700m/700m	1–2	47
2	12hr	3 days	25km/15.4 miles	1370m/1370m	2	51
3	18hr 30min	5 days	38km/23.4 miles	2372m/2822m	2–3	60
4	5hr	1 day	13.2km/8.2 miles	689m/689m	1–2	83
5	3hr 30min	1 day	6.2km/3.8 miles	700m/700m	1–2	88
6	3hr 30min	1 day	7.2km/4.5 miles	570m/570m	2+	92
7	4hr 10min	1 day	9km/5.6 miles	521m/521m	2	98
8	5hr 30min	1 day	10km/6.2 miles	952m/952m	3	100
9	21hr	4 days	46.7km/28.9 miles	3384m/3384m	2+	105
10	3hr 45min	1 day	8km/5 miles	678m/678m	2+	121
11	10hr 30min	2 days	28.2km/17.5 miles	1838m/1838m	2–3	125
12	32hr 30min	7 days	67.2km/41.4 miles	5080m/4878m	2–3	135
13	7hr	1 day	20.2km/12.5 miles	1000m/1000m	1–2	160
14	5hr 20min	1 day	12.2km/7.5 miles	811m/811m	2	165
15	4hr	1 day	9.1km/5.6 miles	862m/862m	2	169
16	6hr 10min	1 day	12.4km/7.7 miles	1209m/1209m	2	173
17	6hr 40min	1 day	14km/8.6 miles	1158m/1158m	2	176
18	5hr	1 day	16.2km/10 miles	928m/1250m	2	180
19	9hr 20min	2 days	21.5km/13.3 miles	1550m/1550m	2+	185
20	4hr 45min	1 day	15km/9.3miles	841m/841m	1–2	193
21	3hr	1 day	7.3km/4.5 miles	500m/500m	1–2	198
22	5hr	1 day	10.5km/6.5 miles	678m/678m	2	202
23	4hr 30min	1 day	9.5km/5.9 miles	1079m/1079m	2	207
24	4hr	1 day	14km/8.7 miles	450m/450m	2	210

NOTES

NOTES

LISTING OF CICERONE GUIDES

BRITISH ISLES CHALLENGES, COLLECTIONS AND ACTIVITIES
The Mountains of England and Wales
  Vol 1 Wales
  Vol 2 England
The UK Trailwalker's Handbook
The Ridges of England, Wales and Ireland
The End to End Trail
The National Trails
Three Peaks, Ten Tors
The Relative Hills of Britain

NORTHERN ENGLAND TRAILS
The Pennine Way
The Spirit of Hadrian's Wall
A Northern Coast to Coast Walk
The Dales Way
Hadrian's Wall Path
The Pennine Way
Backpacker's Britain: Northern England

LAKE DISTRICT
The Mid-Western Fells
The Southern Fells
The Near Eastern Fells
The Central Fells
Great Mountain Days in the Lake District
Tour of the Lake District
Lake District Winter Climbs
Scrambles in the Lake District
  North
  South
The Cumbria Coastal Way
An Atlas of the English Lakes
Rocky Rambler's Wild Walks
Short Walks in Lakeland
  Book 1: South Lakeland
  Book 2: North Lakeland
  Book 3: West Lakeland
The Lake District Anglers' Guide
Roads and Tracks of the Lake District
The Cumbria Way and the Allerdale Ramble
The Tarns of Lakeland
  Vol I: West
  Vol 2: East
Walks in Silverdale and Arnside
Coniston Copper Mines

NORTH WEST ENGLAND AND THE ISLE OF MAN
Walking on the West Pennine Moors
Walking in the Forest of Bowland and Pendle
The Ribble Way
Walks in Lancashire Witch Country
Walking in Lancashire
Isle of Man Coastal Path
The Isle of Man
Historic Walks in Cheshire
Walks in Ribble Country
Walks in The Forest of Bowland
A Walker's Guide to the Lancaster Canal

NORTH EAST ENGLAND, YORKSHIRE DALES AND PENNINES
Walking in County Durham
The Reivers Way
Walking in the North Pennines
The Yorkshire Dales
  North and East
  South and West
Walks in the Yorkshire Dales
The Teesdale Way
The North York Moors
The Cleveland Way and the Yorkshire Wolds Way
Walking in Northumberland
South Pennine Walks
Historic Walks in North Yorkshire
Walks in Dales Country
The Yorkshire Dales Angler's Guide
Walks on the North York Moors
  Books 1 & 2
Walking in the Wolds
A Canoeist's Guide to the North East

DERBYSHIRE, PEAK DISTRICT AND MIDLANDS
White Peak Walks
  The Northern Dales
  The Southern Dales
Historic Walks in Derbyshire
The Star Family Walks
High Peak Walks

SOUTHERN ENGLAND
Walking in the Isles of Scilly
Walking in the Thames Valley
The Cotswold Way
The Lea Valley Walk
Walking in Kent
The Thames Path
The South Downs Way
Walking in Sussex
The South West Coast Path
Walking on Dartmoor
The Greater Ridgeway
London: The Definitive Walking Guide
Walking in Berkshire
The North Downs Way
Walking in Bedfordshire
Walking in Buckinghamshire
A Walker's Guide to the Isle of Wight

WALES AND WELSH BORDERS
Great Mountain Days in Snowdonia
Walking on the Brecon Beacons
Offa's Dyke Path
The Lleyn Peninsula Coastal Path
Hillwalking in Wales
  Vol 1
  Vol 2
Walking in Pembrokeshire
The Shropshire Hills
Backpacker's Britain: Wales
The Pembrokeshire Coastal Path
Ridges of Snowdonia
Hillwalking in Snowdonia

Glyndwr's Way
The Spirit Paths of Wales
Scrambles in Snowdonia
The Ascent of Snowdon
Welsh Winter Climbs

SCOTLAND
Walking on the Orkney and Shetland Isles
Walking on Harris and Lewis
The Isle of Skye
Walking Loch Lomond and the Trossachs
Backpacker's Britain: Central and Southern Scottish Highlands
The Great Glen Way
Ben Nevis and Glen Coe
The Pentland Hills: A Walker's Guide
Walking on the Isle of Arran
Scotland's Mountain Ridges
Walking in Torridon
The Border Country
Backpacker's Britain: Northern Scotland
Walking in the Ochils, Campsie Fells and Lomond Hills
Walking in the Cairngorms
The Southern Upland Way
Scotland's Far West
Walking the Munros
  Vol 1: Southern, Central and Western Highlands
  Vol 2: Northern Highlands and the Cairngorms
Walking in Scotland's Far North
The West Highland Way
Winter Climbs: Ben Nevis and Glencoe
Winter Climbs in the Cairngorms
North to the Cape
Walking the Lowther Hills
The Central Highlands
Walking in the Hebrides
The Scottish Glens
  2: The Atholl Glens
  3: The Glens of Rannoch
  4: The Glens of Trossach
  5: The Glens of Argyll
  6: The Great Glen
Scrambles in Lochaber
Border Pubs and Inns
Walking the Galloway Hills

UK CYCLING
The Lancashire Cycleway
Border Country Cycle Routes
South Lakeland Cycle Rides
Rural Rides No 2: East Surrey
Lands End to John O'Groats Cycle Guide

ALPS: CROSS BORDER ROUTES
Walks and Treks in the Maritime Alps
Tour of Mont Blanc
Chamonix to Zermatt
Across the Eastern Alps: E5
Walking in the Alps

Tour of the Matterhorn
100 Hut Walks in the Alps
Alpine Points of View
Tour of Monte Rosa
Snowshoeing
Alpine Ski Mountaineering
    Vol 1: Western Alps
    Vol 2: Central and Eastern Alps

FRANCE
Mont Blanc Walks
Tour of the Vanoise
Tour of the Oisans: The GR54
The GR5 Trail
Walking in the Languedoc
Écrins National Park
The Robert Louis Stevenson Trail
Tour of the Queyras
The Cathar Way
GR20: Corsica
Trekking in the Vosges and Jura
Walking in the Cathar Region
Walking in the Dordogne
Mont Blanc Walks
Walking in the Haute Savoie
    North
    South
Walking on Corsica
Walking in Provence
Vanoise Ski Touring
Walking in the Cevennes
Walking in the Tarentaise &
    Beaufortain Alps
Walking the French Gorges
Walks in Volcano Country

**PYRENEES AND FRANCE/SPAIN
CROSS-BORDER ROUTES**
The Pyrenean Haute Route
Through the Spanish Pyrenees: GR11
Walks and Climbs in the Pyrenees
The Mountains of Andorra
Way of St James
    France
    Spain
The GR10 Trail
Rock Climbs In The Pyrenees

SPAIN & PORTUGAL
Walking in Madeira
Walking the GR7 in Andalucia
Trekking through Mallorca
Walking in Mallorca
Via de la Plata
Walking in the Algarve
Walking in the Sierra Nevada
Walking in the Canary Islands
    Vol 2 East
Walking in the Cordillera Cantabrica
Costa Blanca Walks
    Vol 1 West
    Vol 2 East
The Mountains of Central Spain
Walks and Climbs in the Picos de
    Europa

SWITZERLAND
Tour of the Jungfrau Region
The Bernese Alps
Walks in the Engadine
Alpine Pass Route

Walking in the Valais
Walking in Ticino

GERMANY
Walking in the Bavarian Alps
Walking the River Rhine Trail
Germany's Romantic Road
Walking in the Harz Mountains
Walking in the Salzkammergut
King Ludwig Way

EASTERN EUROPE
Walking in Bulgaria's National Parks
The High Tatras
Walking in Hungary
The Mountains of Romania

SCANDINAVIA
Walking in Norway

**SLOVENIA, CROATIA AND
MONTENEGRO**
Trekking in Slovenia
The Mountains of Montenegro
The Julian Alps of Slovenia

ITALY
Via Ferratas of the Italian Dolomites
    Vols 1 & 2
Italy's Sibillini National Park
Gran Paradiso
Walking in Tuscany
Through the Italian Alps
Trekking in the Apennines
Walking in Sicily
Walking in the Dolomites
Treks in the Dolomites
Shorter Walks in the Dolomites
Central Apennines of Italy
Walking in the Central Italian Alps
Italian Rock

MEDITERRANEAN
The High Mountains of Crete
Jordan: Walks, Treks, Caves, Climbs
    and Canyons
The Mountains of Greece
Walking in Malta
Western Crete
Treks & Climbs in Wadi Rum, Jordan
The Ala Dag

HIMALAYA
Bhutan
The Mount Kailash Trek
Everest: A Trekker's Guide
Annapurna: A Trekker's Guide
Manaslu: A Trekker's Guide
Kangchenjunga: A Trekker's Guide
Garhwal & Kumaon: A Trekker's and
    Visitor's Guide
Langtang with Gosainkund &
    Helambu: A Trekker's Guide

NORTH AMERICA
The Grand Canyon
British Columbia

SOUTH AMERICA
Aconcagua and the Southern Andes

AFRICA
Walking in the Drakensberg
Trekking in the Atlas Mountains
Kilimanjaro: A Complete Trekker's
    Guide

Climbing in the Moroccan Anti-Atlas

IRELAND
The Irish Coast To Coast Walk
Irish Coastal Walks
The Mountains Of Ireland

EUROPEAN CYCLING
The Grand Traverse of the Massif
    Central
Cycle Touring in Ireland
Cycling the Canal du Midi
Cycling in the French Alps
Cycle Touring in Switzerland
The Way of St James
Cycle Touring in France
Cycling the River Loire
Cycle Touring in Spain
The Danube Cycleway

**INTERNATIONAL CHALLENGES,
COLLECTIONS AND ACTIVITIES**
Europe's High Points
Canyoning

AUSTRIA
Trekking in Austria's Hohe Tauern
Walking in Austria
Trekking in the Zillertal Alps
Trekking in the Stubai Alps
Klettersteig: Scrambles in the
    Northern Limestone Alps

TECHNIQUES
Indoor Climbing
The Book of the Bivvy
Moveable Feasts
Rock Climbing
Sport Climbing
Mountain Weather
Map and Compass
The Hillwalker's Guide to
    Mountaineering
Outdoor Photography
The Hillwalker's Manual
Beyond Adventure
Snow and Ice Techniques

MINI GUIDES
Pocket First Aid and Wilderness
    Medicine
Navigating with a GPS
Navigation
Snow
Avalanche!

For full and up-to-date information
on our ever-expanding list of guides,
please visit our website:
www.cicerone.co.uk.

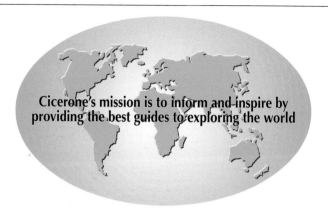

Cicerone's mission is to inform and inspire by
providing the best guides to exploring the world

Since its foundation 40 years ago, Cicerone has specialised in publishing
guidebooks and has built a reputation for quality and reliability. It now
publishes nearly 300 guides to the major destinations for outdoor
enthusiasts, including Europe, UK and the rest of the world.

Written by leading and committed specialists, Cicerone guides are
recognised as the most authoritative. They are full of information, maps
and illustrations so that the user can plan and complete a successful and
safe trip or expedition – be it a long face climb, a walk over Lakeland fells,
an alpine cycling tour, a Himalayan trek or a ramble in the countryside.

With a thorough introduction to assist planning, clear diagrams, maps and
colour photographs to illustrate the terrain and route, and accurate and
detailed text, Cicerone guides are designed for ease of use and access to
the information.

If the facts on the ground change, or there is any aspect of a guide that you
think we can improve, we are always delighted to hear from you.

Cicerone Press
2 Police Square Milnthorpe Cumbria LA7 7PY
Tel: 015395 62069 Fax: 015395 63417
info@cicerone.co.uk www.cicerone.co.uk

CICERONE